THE COON HUNTER'S HANDBOOK

The Coon Hunter's Handbook

LEON F. WHITNEY, D.V.M.

and

ACIL B. UNDERWOOD

Illustrated by ERNEST H. HART

An Owl Book

HENRY HOLT AND COMPANY

NEW YORK

Published by Henry Holt and Company, Inc.,
115 West 18th Street, New York, New York 10011.
Published in Canada by Fitzhenry & Whiteside Limited,
195 Allstate Parkway, Markham, Ontario L3R 4T8.

Library of Congress Catalog Card Number: 52-6636
ISBN 0-8050-1335-0 (An Owl Book: pbk.)

Henry Holt books are available at special discounts
for bulk purchases for sales promotions, premiums,
fund-raising, or educational use. Special editions
or book excerpts can also be created to specification.

For details contact:
Special Sales Director
Henry Holt and Company, Inc.
115 West 18th Street
New York, New York 10011

First published in hardcover by
Holt, Rinehart and Winston in 1952.

First Owl Book Edition—1990

Printed in the United States of America
Recognizing the importance of preserving
the written word, Henry Holt and Company, Inc.,
by policy, prints all of its first editions
on acid-free paper. ∞

1   3   5   7   9   10   8   6   4   2

To B. B. Titus, a coon hunter from "away back" and a man whose friendship has meant so much, this book is affectionately dedicated.

Acknowledgments

The authors hereby gratefully acknowledge the assistance given them by their many coon-hunting friends who contributed suggestions for this book, and especially we thank our wives—those two patient coon-hunting widows—who have put up with our idiocyncrasies and perhaps had to listen to too much conversation about coon dogs and matters appertaining thereto.

We thank Dr. E. G. Fuhrman of the United Kennel Club for his permission to use the copyrighted breed standards of the major coonhound breeds, and the American Kennel Club for the use of the A.K.C. black-and-tan standard.

Dr. William J. Hamilton, Jr., Mr. B. B. Titus, Mrs. George Reid Andrews, Mr. Lurton Blassingame, and Mr. Carl Caulkins deserve special recognition for their help, which is deeply appreciated and acknowledged.

Leon F. Whitney
Acil B. Underwood

Contents

I.	OUR NATIONAL ANIMAL	3
II.	WHAT IS A COON HUNT?	17
III.	QUALIFICATIONS OF A COON DOG	26
IV.	HEREDITY IN THE COON DOG	33
V.	HOUND BREEDS	41
VI.	THE STILL TRAILER	78
VII.	HOW TO OBTAIN A COON DOG	85
VIII.	TRAINING THE COON DOG	97
IX.	HOW TO HUNT COONS	119
X.	COON-HUNTING EQUIPMENT	136
XI.	DISPOSAL OF THE COON	143
XII.	COON-DOG FIELD TRIALS	160
XIII.	HOW TO CONDUCT A FIELD TRIAL	173
XIV.	STANDARD FIELD TRIAL RULES	187
	INDEX	205

THE COON HUNTER'S HANDBOOK

1. *Our National Animal*

THE UNITED STATES has a national bird, the eagle, and a national flower, the goldenrod. We should have a national animal, and we, the authors, nominate for that honor the raccoon.

The raccoon, or arakun, as the Indians called him, is a native of every state of the Union; he has gone hand in hand with our development as a nation; his pelt was even used for money in the early days; and today he beckons a large and growing group of Americans to come outdoors and learn about their countryside.

Yet what does the average American know of the animal, aside from his appearance? He is a small, slow, more or less tough, stupid creature which runs up a tree when a dog barks, lives in swamps, dens only in hollow trees, hibernates, washes everything he eats, lives on frogs, corn in the milk, grapes, and cherries, and whose pelt helps to clothe college students for football games. That's what Mr. Average Man thinks about him; indeed, that's the impression to be gathered from many of our books on natural history. What a pity! For that picture is not only inadequate but inaccurate as well. Most of the information that our people have about the raccoon is actually misinformation.

Our predecessors on this continent, the American Indians, knew the raccoon well. In all their folk tales that featured wit and keenness among the animals they knew, the raccoon outwitted all the rest; and well he might, for there are few, if any, of our native wild animals which exceed the coon in the mental process.

Having studied, raised, and hunted raccoons for years and years, we'd like to debunk some commonly held opinions and show you what an interesting animal he really is.

It has been said that the most desirable type of human being is "the adaptable good sport with a sense of humor." This early American, older than the human race, is the epitome of that definition. And since there is a good possibility the raccoon will some day be our national animal, we should become better acquainted with him.

The word "adaptable" probably describes the most important of the raccoon's characteristics. Had it not been for his adaptability, there would be no such number of coons as there are, no coon hunts, no field trials. Just picture an animal with his wonderful protective coloration (did you ever try to find one in a pine tree at night?) in his native haunts before man came. He had few enemies. Owls, bobcats, larger cats, snapping turtles, and snakes made off with his kittens, but his birth rate was high enough to keep his numbers even. Food was abundant; he was a migrant then, as now, and lived near his food. In the fall he fattened on chestnuts until he tired of them, for the chestnut tree then constituted 68 per cent of the forest population. In the spring he ate high-protein foods consisting of almost anything he could catch from shellfish, fishes, frogs, reptiles, and crawfish to mice, squirrels, rabbits, and bigger game that had been killed and left by larger animals than he. He is so adaptable in his food requirements that it's hard to think of any food eaten by humans that raccoons would refuse.

For years both of us have opened the stomachs of the coons we have taken, and besides finding all the natural foods which you can name, including fruits, nuts, grains, reptiles, fishes, birds, game, and rodents, we have found dill pickles, sour pickles, salami, baked potatoes including the peels, honey, raspberry jam, canned string beans, canned peaches, and poultry. The latter were found in stomachs of coons which had raided garbage pails. The oddest find was a stomach crammed full of fried potatoes cooked in so much mutton tallow that when the cooled remains were turned out for observation the mass was as solid and hard as a candle. That coon had found his meal at a woodchopper's cabin far in the Maine woods. His natural food is almost everything he can get. Like a pioneer, he is adaptable in his menu, and yet, as we'll see later, he shows preferences.

Adaptable in the matter of climate too! The swamp coons of Mexico are thinly furred small animals; the mountain coons are heavier coated and a little larger. As we study the fur of raccoons farther and farther north we find a wonderful adaptability to the environment; the Canadian specimens have such a dense coat—so many hairs to the inch—that they were formerly considered too heavy for coat material and were used only as trimming.

Adaptable in size! Whereas it is a fairly accurate generalization to say that representatives of any well-distributed species—Virginia deer, for example—get larger as they live farther north, that does not apply to the raccoon. Texas coons are among the largest we know, ranking with those of Minnesota and Maine.

Adaptable in the choice of homes! We are talking about animals under natural conditions, unspoiled by man. Here we find that the coon does not live only in hollow trees. In some of the areas he populates, he lives in holes in banks like a woodchuck. He may live in ledges too, or in cliffs. Probably he prefers a den up in a tree, but if he migrates to an area without them, he takes second best and bears it like an adaptable good sport.

Again he typifies the spirit of the pioneers who wore his pelt on their heads for hats.

Self-sufficient! That's another trait of an adaptable human and the adaptable raccoon. He doesn't herd. A female rears her young and educates them without dependence on any other creature; and yet, just as the early pioneer scouts burned with the desire for an occasional glimpse of another human, the raccoon gets around, leaving his solitary existence for a little fraternization now and then.

We really can't appreciate his adaptability until we see what the coming of man meant to the raccoon. Not the Indians; all the coons they could kill with their crude methods could not deplete the numbers. We mean the white man.

White men and Negroes cut down his den trees, plowed up his haunts, dammed his brooks, drained his swamps, usurped his fields for their own communities, filled the country with millions of themselves, brought blight which killed his chestnut trees, and, worst of all, bred dogs for the sole purpose of searching out the coon's tracks and treeing him.

And still the raccoon thrives. Our hats are off to you, Ringtail!

Adaptability again enables him to thrive. "No more or fewer woods' fruits, chestnuts, acorns, beechnuts? O.K.," he says, "I'll eat your corn and your grain. You cut down the chokecherries I love so much because their leaves poison your livestock, and you cut the wild grapes. O.K., I'll climb your fruit trees and your grape vines.

I won't starve. You drained my swamps. O.K. I'll fish your brooks and steal some of the trout you stock them with. You shot off the ruffed grouse whose eggs I loved in spring? I'll rob your hen roosts of eggs and hens too.

"You left me not even a hollow tree in which to raise my young? Then I'll find a hole in a bank like my cousins who always lived in banks, or I'll find a nice little cave in a rock ledge. I'm adaptable.

"You brought parasites and diseases. Lice from your pets sometimes kill me; fleas make me itch. I contract both dog distemper and cat distemper as well as other diseases from your animals.

"You built cities right over my old haunts? I'll move out and come into your gardens in the suburbs and eat your sweet corn and I may eat from your leftovers in the garbage pails."

As a matter of fact, while we have, in a way, turned the world of the poor raccoon upside down, because of his adaptability the coon is actually increasing in many areas, and we can expect even greater increase as long as the value of his pelt is so low that there is little incentive for hunters to kill him. This past season we caught a goodly portion of our coons alive. It's far more fun, anyway. Then we let them go after our season was over, December 31st, which gave them a month and a half to get established and breed.

The coon is adaptable, yes, and he's a good sport too. He honors the feeding ground of another. Study coons in good coon country, say fishing for crawfish along a stream, and you'll not find them ganging up, but each keeping a respectable distance and allowing the others plenty of leeway. At times they seem greedy in captivity, but less so in the wild.

They respect each other's love affairs and a female is interested only in her mate, repelling others. What polygamy there is seems to reside in the males. One of us has often taken a male away from a female and tried to replace him with another, but the female will have none of him. She will probably pace up and down looking through the wire of her cage at her mate, and he will be pacing wanting to join her.

When a coon settles down in her tree, the one she has chosen for her nest, from all we know, the other coons acknowledge it to be her tree and let her have it.

Coons are good sports too in denning up together. Before mating season comes, we have seen six big coons taken by a boy out of a ledge made by a quarry dump. That temporary denning together is not herding, but probably staying together to keep warm.

And a sense of humor! One has but to watch raccoons in play and watch the mother encourage it, pleased as Punch. You can actually see a look of pleasure on the faces. Adults are up to just about as many shines as a monkey.

Now, how do we know? Books of natural history tell us the raccoon is a nocturnal animal. How can one see a coon if he comes out only at night? Because he is not exclusively a night animal. He's often out in the daytime, and in some sections coons are hunted in the daylight. Our captive coons, practically domestic animals, were out by three o'clock many afternoons, and we have also seen a number of wild ones out in the afternoon. We once watched a mother and her young playing in a swamp, and the mother reached down, pulled a walloping Jug-o'-rum bullfrog out, bit it through the head, and gave it to her babies to tug on and eat. Raccoons are not afraid of appearing in daylight.

In fact, a most curious characteristic of the raccoon is that he is not even afraid of and doesn't in the least object to the beam of a strong flashlight played directly on him. If you ever have the opportunity to be on a lake at night, perhaps fishing, and you hear a little noise along the shore, keep quiet, focus your flashlight on the coon making the noise, and leave the light on him. He won't care. He'll go right on with his fishing regardless of the brilliance. One of us has been up a tree and found a mother and her family of four babies out on a limb a little way and just sat there and watched them with the full glare of the light on them. The mother was keenly aware of a human presence, but the five-month-old youngsters scratched themselves and played with each other, completely oblivious of the trouble lurking so close. In that case the trouble let them alone.

One of the very finest studies ever made of raccoons was made at night along a creek with a flashlight. Night after night many coons came to the creek, ate crawfish, and went their way, not one caring for the artificial light held by the naturalist.

How else do books on natural history misinform us? Most blatantly by telling us that the raccoon washes everything he eats. *Procyon lotor* is his name. *Lotor* means the washer. He's even named wrong. As a matter of fact, the raccoon probably washes *nothing* that he eats. We know of no student of natural history who has ever watched a wild raccoon and seen one wash a thing.

Back in 1934 the senior author made a statement in the *Journal of Mammalogy* to this effect. It was radical. It was almost sacrilegious. The raccoon must wash his food; his name is *washer*. The authors of some of the books were nonplussed, but not the careful naturalists; they wanted to know if a common belief was wrong. By one after another the observation has been substantiated. In the wild, the raccoon catches his crawfish and eats it, pulls down an ear of corn and eats it—and no washing.

His name should be *tengador—the feeler,* by virtue of the raccoon's unique characteristic—his uncanny sense of touch. It was because people saw a pet coon feeling of things in his pan of drinking water that they thought he was washing them. But, take away his water and he makes exactly the same motions with the dry object or the article of food. Who hasn't seen a barefoot child purposely stepping in mud or squeezing a handful and letting the slippery stuff ooze between his toes and fingers? Put a pan of crystal clear water and another of slippery mud in the raccoon's cage, and he will "wash" his food in the mud as often as in the water. It feels better when his fingers are wet.

So keen is his sense of feeling that one might say he has eyes in his fingers. He can choose what he wants from a pan of mixed objects by his sense of touch as quickly as he or we can by sight. We have mixed walnuts and stones of the same size and placed the container under a coon's cage which had a hole in the bottom just large enough to reach an arm through. The coon would reach down, touch the tops of the objects, and, not bothering to lift them, snatch out only the nuts.

Fishing for crawfish, he probably can't see them; but he wades around in pools, head up out of the water, moving slowly, deliberately, supporting himself on his hind legs and being supported by the water, feeling with those delicate sense organs until, snap, he's got his crawfish. Or picture him fishing for eels buried in mud along an ocean inlet. Your flashlight tells the story. Here are spear marks where eel fishermen have probed. Here are coon tracks where the animals have sunk so deeply their bellies have dragged in the mud. As deeply as they could reach their hands, they found eels. And then what fun. A tussle! The telltale prints show it.

This delicate, highly developed sense of feeling is noted in the coon's reaction to the slightest movement against his tree or, when captive, his cage wire. He knows at once, via vibrations, when another coon or an enemy is climbing his tree. And yet this sensitivity to feeling is in complete contrast to his reaction to loud noises. Let the lightning flash and the thunder roll—sights and noises which often terrorize dogs—and the coon pays no attention. He may, like one family of raccoons we know, take for an abode a cave in the rock fill of a railroad embankment over which a dozen long freights travel every twenty-four hours. Or he may, like another we knew, find a home under a road where truck traffic, as well as pleasure cars, rolled day and night.

Reports of guns, backfiring of cars, hammering, or any other noises—one never ceases to marvel at how quickly raccoons become adjusted to them—to all but one noise. If a coon is terrified, he emits a scream that conveys the same emotion to every coon nearby. Once a group of us treed five coons in several trees beside a cornfield. By climbing a tree, one of us shook a coon out. Another one of us on the ground caught it by the tail, and a third opened a bag to drop it in. The coon screamed that sharp, piercing, terrified cry of alarm. Zip, every one of those other coons jumped or climbed out and ran away. One was all we got.

Another time we tried to get a large coon out of a hole in the end of a vinegar barrel which held six coons. It seemed impossible. Finally we fixed a loop of sash cord to the end of a stick, slipped it over the nearest one's head, and pulled. The coon screamed, and instead of our getting the coon we held, the other five flew out the opening past us and up the inside of the cage. That noise is one they do mind.

The public receives visual impressions from motion pictures. The general idea that a raccoon is a small animal, slightly larger than a cat, derives from movies and from books which show nothing of familiar size as a basis of comparison. Movies have depicted southern coons mostly. The average mature cat weighs about seven pounds; the average mature southern raccoon is twice as large, but in some sections it is three times as large. We once had this vividly impressed on us while hunting in Maine. Our first trail ran a full mile and we shot a large coon. The next continued at least another mile away from our car, and there we got another coon equally as large. The third ran parallel to the road our car was on, and we got him alive—an even larger specimen. Carrying those three back to the car was a job; together they weighed 78 pounds. We each carried one and took turns with the third. Try carrying even one twenty-five-pound package for two and one half miles through brush and cutover woods, and one coon begins to seem like a very large animal.

People think raccoons are slow because they have seen them waddle across a pen in a zoo. In general, coons do get about in a leisurely manner, but let one decide to get to a certain point and it takes a good hound to catch him. In an open field in full view of a dog, the dog could run him down. Not so in the woods. We have chased one across a field, just about keeping even running as fast as we could. We have had one run down the road in front of a car, really frightened, at twenty miles an hour before hopping aside into the brush. How he ran! Back feet spread out and reaching right up beside his ears, tail up like a bird dog's. You'd call it "high-tailing it" for fair.

We've also seen coons that ran for four hours before treeing. One big three-legged coon ran nearly five hours within ten acres before we got him.

Are you one who believes the coon hibernates? He doesn't. He lives on his fat and sleeps for long periods, but his temperature does not fall as does that of a true hibernating creature—a woodchuck, for example. Warm days followed by warm nights bring him out, and he pokes around. These spells of semidormancy occur at various seasons. We've known most of the coons in a section to den up for the first three weeks in December, be out again until after the January thaw, den up until the first part of February, which is their mating time in the North, and, mating season over, sleep again until warm spring weather and hunger drove them in search of food. This is no more hibernation than a bear's sleep.

The raccoon coats still come out of the moth balls to encase our youths at football games or to be worn in the open convertible, but few are the natural coonskin coats being made today. The fur of the moment is the sheared raccoon. It was discovered that at about one third to one half an inch out from the skin, the color of both the undercoat and the long guard hairs is the same. At this point, too, the coarse guard hair is fine, the coarseness starting beyond that point. Sheared off, then, at just the right length, a fur similar to sheared beaver is the result. No wonder it has mushroomed in popularity. The sheared skin is cut into innumerable narrow strips, and the beautiful, brown, luxurious, durable result is one of the more expensive furs—a feminine fur, no longer a college-boy style.

No evaluation of the raccoon could omit the part this critter plays in sport. Because of the raccoon, every good night in the autumn thousands of Americans are in the woods enjoying the wholesome night air, exercising, and really living. And week ends, out of seasons, these men and others are competing with their dogs in field trials that are probably the most numerous of any field trials today.

And all because of this adaptable good sport which should be our national animal.

2. *What Is a Coon Hunt?*

COON HUNTING in one respect is like politics or religion: a fellow thinks of the kind he knows—the kind he was born into—as the only kind. He often doesn't bother to investigate the other kinds. There are, however, so many types of coon hunting that it's safe to say there is no one standard type.

A coon hunter in Texas may never even have heard of the New England variety. A Virginia swamp coon hunter pictures the sport in a completely different way than the Kansas bluff coon hunter. Why?

The answer: the outstanding attribute common to the hunted and the hunter—adaptability. The raccoon, as we said in Chapter 1, adapts himself to whatever environment he lives in; the hunter uses whatever means he can to catch his game.

We can think of no better way to further portray this quality of adaptability than to sketch the way the animal is hunted in the many sections where he makes his home. The first sketch will describe a coon hunt with all its essentials for the benefit of those who have yet to indulge in their first hunt.

Come with us on a coon hunt that stands out in our memory beyond all others. It was in Maine, not far from the town of Brunswick. One afternoon we saw some coon tracks in shore mud of the Cathance River, but it was eight o'clock when we returned with our dogs to hunt. The night was still, the moon full. Not far away we could hear two foxhounds running a fox. After much working, Bob, one of our dogs, found a track which he ran directly toward the farmhouse where we were staying. Though this did not look any too hopeful, we remembered that we had cut the track of the foxhounds and their fox, so it probably was not a fox that Bob was running. Before we had gone far, we heard Bob barking tree apparently just beside the house across the road from ours. We arrived to find a coon in a cherry tree which drooped over a henhouse. The coon jumped to the top of the house and, with an ease that showed familiarity with the farm buildings, eluded us. By the time the dogs had found his track on the other side of the barn, he was off to the river. The coon ran his best, but could not quite get to the river, and, guided by the dogs, we shot him out of a tree on the bank.

For a while we sat upon a bluff overlooking the river, watching, in the brilliant light of the moon, the dogs working the river bank below. The black dog, TNT, suddenly stood on his hind legs, scenting the air drifts. Then Bob, the white dog, got a whiff. TNT walked out into the cold water, swam to the other shore, and ran up river for a hundred yards. Bob ran along our side of the river; then he too crossed. They began to bay, a stirring duet. We watched intently.

Suddenly our attention was called to something swimming directly toward us, breaking the water and sending out tiny waves. We shone the eyes, which, while not bright, showed much luminescence. It was a coon.

He was losing in his race, for we have never seen dogs swim faster. They bayed as they swam—a music that was in harmony with the witchery of the night, the moon, the frost in the air.

Three quarters of the way across they caught up with the coon. One young man with us knew where a duck boat was pulled upon the shore. We ran to it, pushed it into the river, and all four piled in, though it was meant to carry but two. The fight had gone back to the middle of the river, and Bob was not to be seen. TNT lunged forward and caught the coon by the side of the throat. With that, Bob came to the surface, for the coon had been riding on his head. TNT swam to the far shore;

when we reached him, he had the coon buried in the mud at the water's edge. We dug it up, sloshed it off in the river, threw it in the bottom of the boat, and started back.

The coon must have been shamming, for he picked the middle of the river as a good place to come to life. Craving action, he bit the leg of the heavyweight of the party. The bitten one flared up like a rocket and sought immediate revenge. Up came the skulling oar and down went the butt at the head of the coon, but the coon side-stepped and the butt went through the bottom of the boat. That made trouble and plenty of it. The boat was too jammed for anyone to get out of the coon's way, and everybody had to take his punishment. The heavyweight put a large foot over the hole so the boat didn't go under until we were near enough to the shore to avoid a swim. As it was, the water was above our waists, and the entire party, including coon and dogs, went for the shore under forced draft. The dogs treed the coon after a short chase and he was shot. We returned home to change our clothes and hunted until daylight.

That's coon hunting. You cheerfully endure cold and wet, back-breaking climbs, hours of tramping and running, hoping to find at the trail's end a ringtail up a tree. What would October, November, and December be without this sport? Then, if ever, come perfect nights when you fill your lungs with the vigorous air and down the breeze the chorus of your dogs like "the horns of elf-land, faintly blowing!"

Of course, we might have described a hunt where no

water entered the picture. A great many Maine coon hunts take place in the hills with no more water than one finds in brooks.

In Florida, coon hunts take place both on the beaches and in dryer sections where coons are especially prevalent.

In the calm still night on a Florida beach, some hunters wait until the tide is out. They know that coons walk down on the beach searching for shellfish. After giving them time to arrive, the hunters hurry along the beach, spread out, and shine lights toward the ocean, spotting a coon's eyes. Shouting and running, they drive the animal into the water—the only place he can find protection—and wait at the water's edge while some of their number push a light boat out and row it to the swimming coon. It is no trouble then to catch him alive.

To catch coons in the Florida woods, some hunters do not use dogs, but each carries a five-cell flashlight and one a .22 rifle. Using the lights, they search the moss-draped trees for eyes. Little red beady eyes belong to possums; larger bright reddish eyes belong to coons. We remember one Florida hunt when we found and shot three coons before midnight. Driving home, we saw another waddle across the road and barely escaped striking him. We jumped out, frightened him up a tree, and added him to our booty.

A Michigan coon hunt for drain-tile coons has unique features. The drain-tile coon is one that has been raised in the protective tunnels of drainage systems, which sometimes range over hundreds of acres, and knows every opening in the system. Such coons run to these openings for protection instead of climbing trees.

Our dogs bay first in a drainage ditch. A small trickle of water ripples along, carrying the coon scent from no one knows how far up a drain tile. Our dogs trail up this small stream to the tile and find a coon track leading away, up and over the bank. One of us knows from many hunts where the coon is likely to go. We wait. The dogs are trailing north but circling. They will head for the basin on Baker's land. We run for that tile and sit in front of it, lights out. One of us removes his coat and stuffs it into the fourteen-inch opening of the tile.

We were right. The dogs are heading straight for us now and—what's that?—the scuffling of something not far away, also heading in our direction. In a twinkling it hops over the rim of the basin and tries to crawl into the stoppered tile. For years this big coon has never encountered any obstruction there. Her confusion gives us an opportunity to act. We catch hold of her tail, quickly climb out of the catch basin, and plunge her into a wide-mouthed bran sack just as the dogs arrive ready to attack. Their consternation is as great as was the coon's, but they soon discover her whereabouts from the snarling inside the sack.

As a matter of fact, very few Michigan coon hunts are in the tile-drained country, but we cite this hunt because it helps to establish that the raccoon is an adaptable animal.

A Connecticut coon hunt supports this view further. Taking our dogs to a typical hunting section among the

trap-rock hills, we start them on a brook which flows be
tween tumble-down ledges. The raccoon may be, in the
minds of some, exclusively a tree-dwelling mammal. He
probably once was, but he's certainly not in country
where the only trees are scarcely large enough to give a
squirrel exercise.

Years of hunting experience have told us that a cer
tain ledge, a local name dignifying a pile of jagged
rocks, is the home of coons. It has been ever since we
have hunted that locality. So we lead our dogs to it and
sit down. They have no trouble finding a track, and off
they go to tree the coon, we hope, before he can notice
them and high-tail it for another ledge. But, no, he is
swinging directly back to his home, which he reaches
while we sit powerless to prevent his entering a small
cave in the rocks, fifty yards from where we are. Perhaps
our dogs run five such tracks and tree only one of the
coons. As a matter of fact, during one season our dogs
ran eighty-three coons into ledges and treed twenty-
seven.

How different is such Connecticut hunting from a
Texas coon hunt over great treeless areas. In such country a ringtail's only protection is his endurance and
ability to find a hole. Marshes, streams, and ditches may
confuse the dogs. A group of hunters starts out armed
with a pickax, mattock, shovel, and a lantern or two.
Dogs run the coon until they catch it or until the coon
takes to a hole. Digging is rewarded with either the capture of the coon or the discovery of an armadillo whose
trails coonhounds are wont to follow.

A Georgia coon hunt demonstrates the wonderful ability of coons to travel in shallow or "swimming" water, keeping ahead of dogs. In swamps which no man can travel dry without hip boots, dogs will trail coons for considerable distances, always in packs. Singly a dog may be drowned by a large coon. Keeping on dry land, the hunters follow as closely as they can the progress of the hounds, alternately crossing wide watery areas and standing about a fire to keep warm, until the hounds bark tree. When the hunters arrive, the dogs may be swimming; and when the coon is shot, the splash may soak the hunters. However, a wonderful time will have been had by all.

In some places coons are not exclusively nocturnal. In Virginia coons have been taken with foxhounds at every hour of the day, and coon hunters frequently confine their hunting to daylight hours. A Virginia daytime coon hunt is a popular sport in sections of that state, especially during seasons of full moon. Hunters say that when the moon is bright, the coons stay in their dens at night and come out during the day, "every hour of the day," as one author reports.

Another kind of Virginia daytime hunting is that practiced in marshland. As the same hunter tells us:

"The 'coon bed up in the marsh grass and you jump them just like you jump a fox. It is possible to kill ten or fifteen 'coon a day if one wanted to kill for the lust of killing.

"A good pack of dogs can catch one in from three to twenty minutes after he is jumped; however you stand to lose a dog any time that you go out into the marsh because these marshes are full of ponds and drain ditches, and if your dogs don't know how to fight together the 'coon will drown one."

To hunt coon in any corn-growing state, we park our car on the roadside beside a cornfield and let the dog out. We sit with the windows open and listen for a bark. When the dog trees a coon or catches one on the ground, we go to him and dispatch the coon or take it alive.

From June onward, cornfields may make the principal living grounds for myriads of coons, if the tracks they leave are any indication. One can well imagine their surprise when they start from their dens some night in November to find no protection left and their food gone, except perhaps for stray nubbins or kernels which the cutter and husker lost. Only the shocks of stalks remain, and they are no protection. The amazing point is that the adaptable coon continues to use his fields after the corn is cut and is not frightened to new ones because of the change. When he leaves, it is because of his search for food.

3. *Qualifications of a Coon Dog*

THE IDEAL treehound is a sprightly, energetic, medium-sized hound with hound characteristics but with more verve than most foxhounds possess. Color is a matter of personal choice, but a dog with a preponderantly white coat is preferable for hunting in country with many roads. The coat, though short, is long enough and thick enough to afford protection from the cold.

In height the ideal is about twenty-five inches for

both males and females. The general appearance at side view shows a reasonably square profile except for head and tail. Well-sprung ribs and a deep chest are desirable. The legs are stout with trim ankles, not coarse and heavy. The feet are round—shaped like cat's feet. The hind legs are well angulated at the stifle and hock with the shoulders tight to the body, sloping well and smoothly.

The tail is whiplike with very little flag and carried in a graceful curve high over the back with no tendency to bend downward and forward at the tip.

The head is not too large or cumbersome, tending to be broad and flat on top, not narrow or peaked. There is a furrow between the eyebrows. The eyes are dark brown, not deep-set but large and prominent with a keen yet pleading expression. The foreface is square with lips long enough to produce a rectangle, nose and lower lip lines being parallel. The ears are set on well up on the head in contrast to the bloodhound's ears, which are set on far down the side of the face. They are strong enough to stick out somewhat to the sides when the hound is at attention. The ear tips, without stretching, are just even with the end of the nose.

What then are the necessary qualifications of a true coon dog? Why are good coon dogs so rare and expensive, often bringing prices up to $1,000?

1. A good coon dog must be a natural tree dog. This is the distinguishing mark. Hounds to run any game are very common, but hounds that take to treeing are a different proposition. Even as a pup, the real tree dog will

have the family cat up a tree and make life miserable
for her most of the time. The natural tree dog will tree
squirrels in the daytime. We have known and owned
many natural tree dogs that have been trained to run
fox but instead give up the chase and start treeing squirrels or stray house cats. The natural mental aptitude of
treeing is not so rare, but much rarer than the aptitude
to run after any trail, which most hounds will do.

2. A good coon dog must be a wide ranger. Some
hunters prefer "lantern dogs," which they walk to a
coon track, but the majority expect the dog to do the
hunting after they have taken him to hunting country.
They sit down, tell stories, perhaps smoke, and enjoy
the night with all its beauty of sight and sound.

3. A good coon dog must be a killer and have grit—
not bulldog grit but rather the sagacious variety. He
must not rush headlong into a coon and try to kill it,
because that is equivalent to running right into barbed
wire and gristle. He must be the kind of fighter that
parries for a hold and hangs on after taking hold. Often-
times dogs with badly slashed ears are exhibited. Unscrupulous dog dealers sometimes slash the ears to make
the dogs appear better in the eyes of some unsuspecting
potential buyer. After owning over a hundred coon
dogs, however, we are sure that nearly all of such tears
have been inflicted in dog fights and not by coons. We
nearly always do the climbing and shoot the coon
through the brain. He falls out entirely unconscious
and, although he is shaken by the dog, he suffers no
pain. But then there is grave doubt that a coon and dog

fighting do suffer pain anyway. This is a matter for the psychologists to settle, but we have good reason to believe that very little pain is suffered until after a fight. However, even that little should be avoided, if possible.

4. The good coon dog must have great perseverance and be a sticker at the tree. There's a wide difference between treeing and staying at a tree. We have known tree dogs that stayed and barked tree for twenty-four hours at a stretch. We have often lost our dogs on windy nights and have faintly heard them barking tree, not knowing where they were. Perhaps four to six hours later we have located them.

5. The good coon dog must be good in the water, especially if one hunts near the water often. We have seen several otherwise good dogs drowned or nearly drowned by coons; we hate, therefore, to hunt where there is deep water.

6. He must have a loud voice. Not that a loud voice is imperative in flat country. It isn't. In hilly country, however, it is a must. Small-voiced dogs can get lost from the hunter easily if the terrain is hilly. And certainly it is much more pleasant to listen to a loud, sweet, clear hound note than to a weak yap. Experienced hunters know what it means to have lots of voice in their hounds. We have one whose voice carries three miles on a still night. It is interesting to hear him tree, perhaps a mile away along with other dogs whose voices do not carry so far. It sounds as if only one dog is barking tree, but as we approach we hear a second and finally a third, after we have cut the distance to half a mile.

7. A good coon dog must have a pleasant voice. This is not necessary to the blood hunter, but to the sportsman it is one of the chief elements of a truly happy hunt. What old hunter can't close his eyes and still hear the lovely strains of hound music floating across a valley or stream. Surely no man-made music can light the fires of imagination or bring a greater thrill of delight than can a hunter's best friend—his hound.

8. A good coon dog must be powerful physically. This too can be modified, because there are small hounds which indeed get the game. We are talking about an ideal, if it is to be had.

9. He must be willing to hunt nothing but tree-living animals. This is the one requirement that disqualifies most field-trial dogs. It is the one thing that causes more heartaches to the owners of dogs than anything else. One year one of us was determined that, if we were going to pay as much as $150, we would buy a dog that would hunt nothing but coon. So we found a spot where the deer yarded and another place where there were three separate fox dens. There were always fox or deer where we could find them easily. When the dog came, we tried him out in this country first; and a week later the shipper in Missouri had him back again. We tried dogs from all over the Middle West and South, having tried ten dogs by the middle of the hunting season. Not one of them was deer-proof, and few were fox-proof.

We became desperate. We challenged a man to ship us a good dog or else pay the express charges. He did so.

The dog came, a thin scrawny dog that hadn't had a good meal in goodness knows how long. We fed him well and let him have two days in which to rest. He seemed to take a real fancy to us, too. Then we set him loose in the deer country. He left us and was gone half an hour. We began to think we were out one hound-dog. But, just as we were getting uneasy, we heard him bay off beyond where we thought he was. He came directly toward us, and we stood up and took a deep breath, on the verge of yelling to try and stop him. The dog was within fifty yards of us when what should go dashing by but a coon, not over ten feet away. We sat down, let out our breath, and listened to the dog tree him about fifty feet from us. We kept that dog, and he became famous. When he died, we had letters of sympathy from a dozen hunters. He had been the father of many fine coon dogs; he had accounted for over a hundred coons and many squirrels; and he had won his way into the hearts of all the hunters of our locality and everywhere else he was known.

No one who has not experienced the feeling can quite realize what it means to a coon hunter to go into the woods, hear his dog start the game, listen to him as he drives up a brook, and then wait in vain for the dog to tree. All he hears is the sound of trail-barking, and he realizes that the dog is chasing a deer or a fox. It is very difficult to break a coon dog from running either of these animals. Both leave strong scents, and the dogs have never had experience with them before.

Besides deer and fox, there are other animals which a

good coon dog should not touch, among these bobcats and porcupine, although some hunters want their dogs to tree them. The bobcat can be found in scattered sections all over the United States. The porcupine is found only in the North and represents a real problem to coon dogs and coon hunters alike. This will be discussed in a later chapter.

10. A good coon dog must be in good health. Come August or September, the wise hunter takes a specimen of his dog's stool to the veterinarian and asks for a centrifuged fecal examination to determine whether the dog is infested with internal parasites. If infestaiton is present, he has the dog dewormed. He also has the stool studied for tapeworm segments. He keeps the dog's skin free from infection and insect infestation. He cuts the dog's nails. He has his hounds vaccinated against distemper and exercises them before the season opens so that they are in hunting trim with tough feet and no surplus fat.

4. *Heredity in the Coon Dog*

TODAY IN UP-TO-DATE high schools and colleges, students are taught in biology or genetics courses the ABC's of heredity. You probably remember how the mechanism of inheritance operates, but a brief review may be helpful before we take up the actual, known, hereditary traits of the coon dog.

Every individual is produced by the architectural plan latent in the germ plasm. Your plasm carries the plans for a human being; a cucumber's germ plasm carries the plans for a cucumber vine and fruit; a redbone coonhound's germ plasm determines that he won't be a bulldog.

Every individual characteristic in the body is determined by a chemical packet in the germ plasm so tiny that only electron microscopes can make it visible. It is called a gene. There are a pair of genes for each characteristic, and some characteristics have many pairs. Blue-ticking is probably determined by only one pair of genes. A dog's ability to run fast is the product of many genes.

The genes, with certain exceptions, always function in pairs. They are held together in long strings by some invisible means. The strings are called chromosomes. Each chromosome, containing a great many genes, pairs with another similar chromosome. On one chromosome may be a gene which determines that a dog be brindle; on the other, a gene for the lack of brindling.

When the sperm (male reproductive) cells are formed, there is a split between every pair of chromosomes so that one goes into one sperm cell and the other into another one. The chromosomes determining sex, called X and Y chromosomes by biologists, differ in males and females. Males have one chromosome of each type, or XY; females have chromosomes of only one type, or XX.

The female reproductive cells or eggs (called ova by biologists), contain two X chromosomes as just stated; but before the eggs unite with the sperm cells to form a new individual, each egg spews out one whole set of chromosomes.

Now, since half the sperm cells carry X chromosomes and the other half Y, and since all the eggs carry X, it is plain that it is a matter of chance which sex any pup will be at conception. Half should be males and half females. However, many pups die as embryos and the sex ratio of pups at birth is about 120 males to each 100 females, with variations. Each puppy gets half its characteristics from its dam and half from its sire through nature's ingenious method.

Often traits seem to skip a generation. A bluetick hound may mate with a tricolor and produce no tricolors at all among the puppies. How can this be explained? Why do blends or half shades of color seem to occur so seldom? The puppies are either blueticked or they are not; they are either brindle or not.

The explanation of all of these problems lies in the fact that a dog can carry both genes, but one completely dominates the other. The one that dominates is called the dominant, and the dominated one is called the recessive. The gene for blueticking is dominant; that for the absence of it is recessive.

How can a pair of blueticks produce an unticked pup? Does blueticking skip a generation? No, it only seems to. This is what happens.

Let's represent the ticking gene by T and the gene for no ticking by t. A pure blueticked hound TT is mated with a pure nonticked hound tt. The sperm cells of the sire will each carry one T. The eggs of the mother have only t. A sperm joins its chromosomes with those of the egg, and now each new individual has Tt. The T is dominant, so all the puppies, male and female, will look blueticked and have no half shades.

These pups grow up, and a brother and sister are mated. Out of 100 pups, what could we expect? Half the sperm cells of their father would carry a T; the other half, a t. The same would apply to the mother's eggs—half would carry T, the other half, t. All we have to do is figure out how they could join. The following combinations would be possible: TT, Tt, and tt. Mathematically the numbers would be 25 per cent TT, 50 per cent Tt, and 25 per cent tt.

The TT would be pure blueticks; the Tt would be half-bred blueticks like the parents—they would look blueticked; and the tt would not be blueticked at all. They would appear to have skipped a generation. That's how these characteristics are inherited. Many traits, however, are not so simple, because they are determined by many pairs of genes in the germ cells.

Those which, to the best of present-day knowledge, are determined by one pair of genes are as follows:

DOMINANT PARENT	RECESSIVE PARENT	EXPECTATION
	Color	
Black	All other colors	Black
Solid color	Ringneck pattern	Solid color
Solid color	Mostly white	Solid color
Ringneck	Mostly white	Ringneck
Black-and-tan	Tricolor	Black-and-tan
Black-and-tan	Liver-and-tan	Black-and-tan
Black-and-tan	Red (type I)	Black-and-tan
Red (type II)	Black-and-tan	Red (type II)
All colors	Albino-white	All colors
All colors	Dark-eyed white	All colors
Brindle	Tan	Brindle
Black-and-brindle	Black-and-tan	Black-and-brindle
Lemon-black nose and dark eyes	Lemon-pink nose and light eyes	Lemon-black nose and dark eyes
Ticking	Nonticking	Ticking
Merling	Tricolor	Merling
Merling	Black-and-tan	Merling
Sable	Black-and-tan	Sable
Sable	Merling	Sable
Red	Cream	Red
Red	Isabella	Red

DOMINANT PARENT	RECESSIVE PARENT	EXPECTATION
	Leg Length	
Short legs (imperfectly)	Long legs	Short legs (imperfectly)
Long legs	Short legs in cockers	Long legs
	Eye Color	
Brown eye	Yellow eye	Brown eye
Brown eye	Pearl eye	Brown eye
	Coat Characteristics	
Short hair	Long hair	Short hair
Wire coat	Smooth coat	Wire coat
Coarse hair	Fine hair	Coarse hair
Sparse coat	Dense coat	Sparse coat
Straight	Curly	Straight
	Mental Aptitudes	
Open trailing	Still trailing	Open trailing
Chop voice	Drawling voice	Chop voice
High head carriage in hunting	Low head carriage	High head carriage in hunting
Smiling	Nonsmiling	Smiling
Bird interest	Lack of bird interest	Bird interest
Watergoing	Nonwatergoing	Watergoing
Quartering	Straight-line hunting	Quartering
	Miscellaneous	
Dew claws	No dew claws	Dew claws
Stub tail (imperfectly)	Long tail	Stub tail (imperfectly)
Straight tail	Curly tail	Straight tail
Glaucoma	Normal sight	Glaucoma
Shorter ears	Longer ears	Shorter ears

With these facts in mind, let's suppose we are going to embark on a breeding program to produce a certain type of dog. Shall we just blindly make matings and hope for the best, or shall we plan on the basis of genetic knowledge? If we follow the latter course, we shall

succeed quickly. If we follow the former, we'll find ourselves senselessly breeding animals as our forefathers
did, relying on superstition and such nonsense. now
time-tested and negated, as:

The idea that one mating influences those which
follow. If a fine bitch, in earlier days, was mated acci-
dentally to a cur, then she had as well be shot; her use-
fulness as a breeder had ended. That's all wrong! The
mating would not hurt her one iota as a breeder.

The idea that animals are *blood relatives*. Blood is
not inherited. The term "bloodlines" is foolish. Don't
use it. The animal starts life as two cells and no blood.
It makes its own, and inheritance is in no way via blood
but via genes and chromosomes.

The idea that bitches can mark their offspring. One
sometimes hears such remarks as, "Hunt 'em hard while
they're carrying pups; the pups'll be better hunters," or,
"If a bitch is scared by something, her pups will be
nervous." There is absolutely nothing to the birth-
marking bugaboo.

The idea that acquired characteristics are inherited.
If a dog is hunted all its life and is trained to be a great
dog, this old idea would have us believe that his pups
will inherit the ability he acquired. But if it works one
way, it should work the other—dogs must become worse
generation after generation by not exercising their
capacities. We know they do not. The exercise and training and field trials give us a chance to choose the best
from which to breed, but puppies are not better because
their sires and dams were trained.

It may interest you to know how all these differences in our breeds and dogs within breeds came about, if not by inheriting acquired characteristics. We know that sudden changes in the germ plasm occur all the time. These are known as mutations. In the evolutionary scheme, some mutations are in an upward direction and some downward. A white pink-eyed dog—an albino—would be downward. So would a screw tail on a redbone. But a thirty-inch ear spread in a black-and-tan from a strain which had never before produced more than a twenty-four-inch ear spread would be a mutation in the right direction as far as black-and-tan breeders are concerned. Mutations are appearing all the time, perhaps at a rate of one in a thousand individuals.

A useful mutation may occur in one of your dogs. Always be on the lookout, for you never know when it will happen. Breed the best to the best, not to the most convenient; better not to breed at all than to breed to inferior stock. The great significant changes in our dog breeds have come about by breeders taking advantage of mutations and breeding dogs which showed them until the new or improved character was incorporated in the strain. They did not come from the inheritance of acquired traits.

If you want to be a successful dog breeder, forget the false ideas enumerated above and adopt the scientific approach. Apply it to everything you've believed, to what's been told you, to all your actions. When it was applied to the old ideas above, they had to be junked because they couldn't stand scrutiny. What is the scientific method? Just this:

Never twist the facts around to fit your own theory; instead, test your theory in every possible way and let the findings support or invalidate it. The former is nothing more than rationalizing; the latter is honest thought. Get the habit.

Let's apply this method to dog breeding and examine a commonly held opinion: If the coat of a Shepherd is clipped twice a year for field trials, the hair will come in coarser.

We then make two parallel columns, one labeled "Plus" and the other "Minus." We do not say, "Certainly, that's true," and proceed to write down all the facts we can find to prove what we think. No, we try just as hard to find the facts on the negative side. After we have assembled and interpreted the data, we state what the facts show. In this case, we would probably have to state that there are not enough real facts to answer the question. All we could rely on would be opinions.

Reliance upon opinions was what held dog breeding back. Not until the application of the scientific method did dog breeding make the rapid strides in evidence today.

5. *Hound Breeds*

SINCE OUR EARLY ancestors learned the value of the dog in taking raccoons, there has been steady evolution toward perfecting dogs as an instrument of man in capturing the animal for meat and fur as well as for enjoyment. At first the farm shepherd dog sufficed. Shepherds are still often expert coon dogs. But with the importation of foxhounds and bloodhounds, crosses were made—nobody knows how many or just what kinds.

Men in separate localities developed strains of dogs

which varied around different standards. One man
would own an outstanding cooner and everybody who
enjoyed coon hunting would breed his bitch to this
best dog. The man himself would keep some bitches
and evolve a type of his own. In many instances the dogs
he started with were the products of several strains or
breeds of many colors. After a number of decades the
strains would become individualized and advertised
until they were known as Redbones, Birdsongs, Triggs,
black-and-tans, and others. In later years correspondence
and personal communication through travel brought
together men who agreed on what an ideal coonhound
should look like and be like, and dogs were shipped
considerable distances for the purpose of breeding.

Now we have a number of subbreeds of coonhound,
each of which is becoming individualized. One—the
black-and-tan—has been recognized by the American
Kennel Club, and others are recognized by other reg-
istry associations. So far the various subbreeds are dif-
ferentiated chiefly on the basis of color, although there
are other differences by which these types can be identi-
fied, as you will see. Some are foxhound breeds which
have been converted to coon hunting by selection of
dogs from the foxhound stock. These breeds have been
emancipated by some hereditary mutation from fox
hunting, preferring treeing to mere trail running. Of
these the black-and-tan and the treeing Walker are the
best examples. The old-fashioned black-and-tans were
foxhounds long before they were bred for treeing. Just
as all the dogs of the bird-hunting group of breeds are

primarily interested in birds, so all of the typical dogs of the coon hound breeds are interested in tree-living animals.

If you look at the best of these breeds, you will notice a similarity of type. At field trials you may see dogs of different breeds winning, yet you cannot help but observe that if they were all the same color they would appear to be of the same breed, with some variations, of course. There are, however, variations within any breed.

The authors have been fortunate in owning dogs of all the various breeds and can be entirely impartial in their evaluation. Good ones of each breed are wonderful animals; poor ones of each are not worth owning.

If you decide to breed coonhounds of one particular color, help to make that breed sufficiently unlike any of the others that in time it becomes distinctive. You can then point with pride to the fact that you are a breeder of treeing Walkers or Redbones or whatever breed you fancy. That's the way to have the most fun in the coonhound game.

The following breed descriptions will help to point out the differences between breeds as they exist today. The breed standards define the ideals which breeders are striving to achieve.

What we are going to say about the breeds of coonhounds will not please everybody. Every pamphlet or magazine we have seen which discusses the various breeds, or types, as we prefer to call them, has been filled with wild guesses and vague statements as to the origin of each breed. All of them sooner or later trace the breeds back to George Washington's or Lafayette's hounds in Virginia, to bloodhounds, or to English foxhounds. How many tell about the magnificent shepherd-dog crosses of which there were doubtless many?

The truth is that we don't know the exact lineage of a single type of coonhound bred today. Therefore, it is useless to waste pages in describing the ancestry as read from a magazine article in which a man wrote what he had read in another magazine.

Take, as an example, the so-called English coonhound. There is a real English foxhound. It is a heavy, straight, thick-legged pack hound which stands high on its feet, about as different from the English coonhound as it could be. What one of us learned years ago about the true origin of the English coonhound as repeated by a very old settler is at complete variance with the story that has been told and retold about the type.

Our story, in which we have confidence, is that back in the early days of the settlement of Johnson County, Arkansas, the Cazort family brought with them a long, trim, bluetick hound and a true English tricolor. One was a dog and one a bitch. Both had glorious voices. These two dogs were the ancestors of many of the early settlers' coon dogs. They were inbred and occasionally outcrossed, but the two distinct types kept occurring. The bluetick color was no respecter of types and sometimes appeared on the English type and sometimes on the lithe type. In the mountains one still finds both types, with variations between.

One day in 1925, one of us was at Ozone, Arkansas, and there saw a bluetick of the lithe sort. On investigation it was learned he had a brother of the English type. Both were bought. Their voices were nearly identical, but their forms were unlike, the true English foxhound traits having apparently persisted for over a hundred years.

We read that Redbones were once black-and-tan in color. Another "authority" may say that they were redticked and blueticked. One author says that Mr. Redbone originated them; another says that somebody else did. The same is true in the case of treeing Walkers. Probably they have no relationship to true Walker foxhounds and often little resemblance, except for color, to that strain of fast foxhounds. Those we have owned were red-and-white and tricolored hounds which somebody had called treeing Walkers. This, by the way, did not detract one iota from our esteem of them as coon hunters.

We are, then, purposely going to neglect the hazy background of history and tell about the breeds as we know them.

The Black-and-Tan

A good looking black-and-tan hound presents one of the loveliest pictures of all dogdom. The sparkling gloss on the jet black saddle, the pumpkin-seed yellow or mahogany dots over the eyebrows, the long low-set velvety ears, the keen, penetrating dark hazel eyes which appear to convey complete understanding, and the whip tail which is carried proudly over the back when its owner is in action make a combination hard to beat. The true black-and-tan stands but one step below the bloodhound, for it was the bloodhound that our forebears considered the acme of hound perfection. They named it the bloodhound to express the idea of "blooded hound," for in those days people spoke of heredity in terms of blood.

No bloodhound has the earage of the best black-and-tans, even though the latter got their principal distinctive features from the former. Many consider the black-and-tan a more beautiful breed than the bloodhound. Indeed, one might say it is a smaller, lithe, and graceful bloodhound. People especially like the tight eye of the black-and-tan in contrast to the somewhat repulsive red haw of the droop-eyed breed.

Black-and-tans love trailing as much as any breed alive, and they do it well. In the early days of America the black-and-tan was the individual hunter that ran his own fox and cared nothing about packing, as the true English foxhound does. A pack of black-and-tans is almost useless for riding to, because of their independent temperaments. Each will let the other hounds run their foxes while he runs his own. When one hears stories of a foxhound running a fox across ice where other hounds can't follow, one generally learns the dog was a long-eared hound and nearly always typically black-and-tan. Almost all of the breed were used for fox hunting.

The Yankee fox hunter who was taken on an English

fox hunt was the owner of a black-and-tan, you may be sure. He was used to carrying his gun over his arm and listening for his dog so that he could be in the proper place to shoot the fox when it appeared. However, when he arrived to go fox hunting with the nobility, he was dressed in the proper riding costume and rode off as proudly as anyone. The fox was soon jumped by the pack, and the Yankee reached instinctively for his gun, which wasn't there, of course, yelled something, and dug his spurs into his horse to lead the chase. That evening at the ball following the hunt he was completely shunned by men and women alike, a fact for which he could not account. Seeking an explanation, he asked his host, "Am I not properly attired? Was I not properly attired for the hunt? Did I break some rule?"

"Ah, no," his host replied. "It is not that, but rather what you shouted when the fox was first sighted. Our custom is to shout, 'Tally-ho! The fox!,' not 'There goes the son-of-a-bitch!' "

Coon hunters have trained and bred the black-and-tan away from fox hunting toward coon hunting. The early black-and-tans were usually about three-quarters-leg length. Today this type continues to be bred by many fox hunters, but coon hunters and show enthusiasts breed the dogs for long legs and speed. Fox hunters who hunt to hear the chase seldom use black-and-tans at all, but some fox hunters use both the long- and short-legged types to drive foxes that they shoot. We have known many black-and-tans of this short-legged type with a quality in their voices that foxes or coons did not fear. The steady, if slow, pursuit, even cadence, and un-varying tone seem to lull the game into a loss of fear. Often the fox will be no more than a hundred yards ahead of the dog; the coon will tree quickly. Naturally owners of such hounds could cut a good many notches on their sticks for pelts with which to credit their hounds. If one of the big-voiced black-and-tans with the long legs of modern breeding was turned in after any fox, the fox would have to move to keep ahead.

The coon hunters' hounds are often of a different sort mentally from those of the fox hunters. Through selective breeding and training, they are tending to become straight cooners. Still, many of the show black-and-tans should not be registered as coonhounds, as the American Kennel Club records them, for they are used as foxhounds par excellence.

No breed can boast such magnificent voices in such a high proportion of their dogs as the black-and-tan. There are few of these typical hounds with chop voices; most of them bawl, and that bawl is music. Not all their voices have the lovely quality of those of some other breeds, being somewhat coarser; but theirs are full-volumned voices which carry well. At the tree the voices tend to lose their drawl and to chop steadily. The contrast helps in determining when the dogs have treed.

Trainers find the true type of black-and-tan somewhat stubborn and harder to break from deer, fox, and rabbits than many other types of coonhound. They are often hard-headed and perhaps not quite as responsive as they could be; but once they are broken they do not tend to leave off running coon and go back to running trash—the coon hunters' name for other types of game. It is claimed that the night-dog type of black-and-tan is less stubborn; certainly this type seems further removed from the bloodhound and more like the most successful night dogs of other breeds.

Today, and not without justification, there are two definite types of black-and-tan. One is the variety we have just been describing; the other is the tightly knit, shorter eared, sleek, fast, speed type with the arched back. It resembles not the true black-and-tan, as called for by the A.K.C. standard, but rather the kind of hound which wins at the field trials. Put a tricolor coat on it and you might have a treeing Walker. Put a bluetick factor in the white coat and you would have a speedy bluetick.

A great many proponents of this type scoff at the thirty-inch ear spread toward which the show-type people are breeding. Such ears, they say, are absurd on a night dog. Many breeders are even advertising that their hounds are like the black-and-tan standard but have "sensible ears." Actually, the difference between the fast type and the show black-and-tan is as great as that between the show black-and-tan and the Redbone. It was a great blow to the sincere hunters who had given years to the development of their strains when the "long-eared" faction joined the A.K.C. as a member club and set the standard. Many feel that the long-eared type should continue to be bred for foxhounds, in which ears are not a detriment, and that a breed of short-eared black-and-tans should be patterned solely for night hunting. The success of the short-eared type advocates in selling pups is some indication that we may have two types of black-and-tans in the future as in the past.

AMERICAN BLACK-AND-TAN STANDARD: OFFICIAL U.K.C.

The breeders and fanciers who were greatly responsible for this standard are: Mr. J. W. Street, Mr. Errol Draffen, Mr. M. B. Guin, and Mr. C. Z. Bennett who organized and carried ever forward the United Kennel Club, Inc., and by their loyal efforts and that of the breeders placed the American Black-and-Tan Coonhound on the high standard it now enjoys and will continue to enjoy.

Head and Neck. Head carried well up, dome shaped, occiput bone prominent, plenty of width between and above eyes. Ears set low, thin, narrow, soft, hanging in a roll, no erectile power. Eyes dark, prominent, no drooping eyelids, muzzle square and deep, rather long. Large open nostrils black and not butterfly or pink.

Neck not too thick nor too long, but graceful and strong, free of dewlap.

Shoulders. Muscular and sloping. Indicating speed and strength.

Chest. Deep, moderately wide, showing large lung space.

Back. Short and slightly arched, well muscled and strong. This is one important part of this breed—strong short back, not roached. A good rule to breed to is same distance from root of tail to shoulder as height at shoulder.

Hips. Smooth, round, proportionately wide, flanks gracefully arched, muscular, and loins, tail, heavy, strong at root, tapering there, rather long without brush, carried free, well up, saberlike.

Legs—Front. Straight, smooth, forearm muscular. Straight at knees, perfectly in line with upper leg.

Legs—Hind. Strong and muscular above hock, slightly bent at hock, no cow hock.

Feet. Round, solid, cat foot, well padded and knuckled, set directly under leg. This is a very important part in this breed.

Color and Coat. Smooth haired, fine glossy, but thick enough for protection. Deep rich black, with dark tan. Small pumpkin seed over eyes. A little white on breast is not a fault. But no white is preferable. No white on feet or tip of tail under any circumstances.

Voice. Open, deep, free bugle, bawl, but not choppy.

Height. Slightly more at shoulders than at hips. Males: 23 to 25 inches. Females: 22 to 24 inches.

Weight. Males: 50 to 60, females: 40 to 60 pounds.

Length of Muzzle. Males: 9 to 10 inches from occiput bone to end of nose. Females: 8 to 9 inches from occiput bone to end of nose.

Ear Spread. About the same as height at shoulder. Males: 23 to 25 inches, not flat and stiff or set high. Females: 22 to 24 inches.

Characteristics of This Breed. Active, fast, bright, kind, confident, courageous, with great trailing and treeing instinct and ability.

Points

Head	10
Neck	5
Shoulders	10
Chest and Ribs	10
Back and Loins	15
Hind Quarters	10
Elbows	5
Legs and Feet	20
Coat and Collar	5
Stern	5
General Make-up	5
	100

(As adopted by the Black and Tan Coonhound Club of America and approved by the Board of Directors of the American Kennel Club at the meeting held July 10, 1945.)

The black-and-tan coonhound is first and fundamentally a working dog, capable of withstanding the rigors of winter, the heat of summer, and the difficult terrain over which he is called upon to work. Judges are asked by the Club sponsoring the breed to place great emphasis upon these facts when evaluating the merits of the dog.

The general impression should be that of power, agility, and alertness. His expression should be alert, friendly, eager, and aggressive. He should immediately impress one with his ability to cover the ground with powerful rhythmic strides.

Head. The head should be cleanly modeled, with medium stop occurring midway between occiput bone and nose. The head should measure from 9 to 10 inches in males and from 8 to 9 inches in females. Viewed from the profile the line of the skull is on a practically parallel plane to the foreface or muzzle. The skin should be devoid of folds or excess dewlap. The flews should be well developed with typical hound appearance. Nostrils well open and always black. Skull should tend toward oval outline. Eyes should be from hazel to dark brown in color, almost round and not deeply set. The ears should be low set and well back. They should hang in graceful folds giving the dog a majestic appearance. In length they should extend well beyond the tip of the nose. Teeth should fit evenly with slightly scissors bite.

Body. Neck, Shoulders and Chest: The neck should be muscular, sloping, medium length, extending into powerfully constructed shoulders and deep chest. The dog should possess full, round, well-sprung ribs, avoiding flatsidedness.

Back and Tail: The back should be level, powerful, and

strong, with a visible slope from withers to rump. Tail should be strong, with base slightly below level of back line, carried free, and when in action at approximately right angles to back.

Legs and Feet: The forelegs should be straight, with elbows well let down, turning neither in nor out; pasterns strong and erect. Feet should be catlike with compact, well-arched toes and thick, strong pads.

Hind Quarters: Quarters should be well boned and muscled. From hip to hock long and sinewy, hock to pad short and strong. Stifles and hock well bent and not inclining either in or out. When standing on a level surface the hind feet should set back from under the body, and leg from pad to hock be at right angles to the ground when viewed both from profile and the rear. The stride of the black-and-tan coonhound should be easy and graceful with plenty of reach in front and drive behind.

Coat and Color. The coat should be short but dense to withstand rough going. As the name implies, the color should be coal black, with rich tan markings above eyes, on sides of muzzle, chest, legs, and breeching with black pencil markings on toes.

Size. Measured at the shoulder, males 25 to 27 inches. Females 23 to 25 inches. Height should be in proportion to general conformation so that dog appears neither leggy nor close to the ground. Dogs oversized should not be penalized when general soundness and proportion are in favor.

Judges should penalize the following defects: Undersize, elbows out at shoulder, lack of angulation in hind quarters, splay feet, sway or roach back, flatsidedness, lack of depth in chest, yellow or light eyes, shyness and nervousness.

Faults: Dewclaws; white on chest or other parts of body is highly undesirable and if it exceeds 1½ inches in diameter should be disqualified.

The Redbone

Of all types of coonhound, none is as uniform as the Redbone. If a hunter wishes to buy a pup with the greatest assurance of getting a real cooner, his best bet is one of the Redbone breed. By this we mean real Redbones, bred by reputable breeders who have the interests of the breed at heart. *The real Redbone type is the most uniform of all.*

Almost in the same breath we must warn that unscrupulous dealers and those ignorant of coon-dog types call practically all red coonhounds Redbones. We are not discussing red hounds here. Please observe the illustration and you will see what a real Redbone looks like. Observe all the red hounds and even red mongrels which you have been told were Redbones, and the differences become apparent. The breed is distinguished not only by color and form but also by a kind expression in the eye which completely belies the Redbone's passion for hunting.

In form the Redbone gives the appearance of a well-balanced, not particularly long-legged breed with the look of the bloodhound about him. Some of the breeders are selecting for long legs and speed, but the substantial breeders are interested primarily in brains and hunting sagacity, while keeping the type uniform. The ears are not low hung; when the dog is at attention, the ear flaps seem to join the skin of the head at about the uppermost point of the flattish top. The standard calls for a "pleading expression" in the eyes, and this term describes it perfectly. No breed of hound shows the kindness of the Redbone.

The dogs are not bred for great size. We never saw one over twenty-six inches, although there have been some. The coat tends to be harsh rather than silky and is not scanty. Redbones stand the cold admirably.

Uniformity in voice is notable. Most Redbones have a sweetness and "come on" in their tone that is extremely pleasant to the ear. The Redbone's notes are shorter than the organlike tones of the black-and-tan, but they are just as well remembered. Redbones we have owned have sung to us in tones we can still hear. They were all among the top cooners we have owned.

One seldom finds a Redbone that potters. While many dogs of other types seem to enjoy the scent so much that they don't care whether they ever get to the tree, the Redbones seem determined to get the coon. Their tree bark is usually a chop voice of loud and pleasant quality.

Redbones are most uniform in size. Occasionally one finds small, wiry, purebred dogs in field trials; but even they, when fattened, are typical. In fact, they are more typey than representatives of other types are in comparison with their standards.

REDBONE COONHOUND STANDARD: OFFICIAL U.K.C.

This standard was drafted by the Redbone Breeders Association at the meeting held in 1949 at Anderson, Indiana. There was little change from the old U.K.C. standard.

This standard was drafted for two real purposes:

1. To act as a guide for the U.K.C. and its judges at bench shows.

2. To furnish suggestions for the breeders in their aims toward improving the breed to higher ideals in their breeding.

Color. Solid red preferred, small amount of white on blanket or feet not objectionable.

Head. Ears set moderately low, fine in texture, not stiff and reaching near the end of the nose when stretched out. Ears in proportion to head. Fault: Ears not firmly attached to head, seemingly just to skin.

Eyes brown or hazel in color, dark eyes preferred. Set well apart and of pleading expression.

Skull moderately broad, well proportioned with body.

Muzzle well balanced with other features of head, never dished or upturned.

Teeth even, neither over- nor undershot.

Neck. Throat clean, medium in length, strong, slightly arched and held erect denoting proudness. Slight fold of skin below angle of jaw not objectionable.

Size. Slightly taller at shoulder than at hips. Never opposite. Males 22 to 26 inches. Females 21 to 25 inches.

Body. Deep broad chest, back strong and slightly arched, length well proportioned to height, thighs and shoulders up, clean and muscular. Well-sprung ribs, plenty of lung space.

Legs. Legs straight, well boned, pasterns straight, well set, clean and muscular denoting combination of both strength and speed. Never cow hocked.

Feet. Cat-paw type, compact, well-padded toes strong and well arched, stout well-set nails. Feet should set as directly under leg as possible.

Tail. Medium in length, very slight brush, carried gaily but not hooked over back. Set moderately high.

Coat. Smooth and hard, medium to short in length, sufficient for protection.

Manners. A hound should always indicate a willingness to obey his master's command which denotes intelligence.

Voice. While voice is an important factor in the hound, it should not be considered in bench shows but only on trail or at the tree.

The Ticked Breeds

Of the three major types (including black-and-tan and Redbone), the bluetick, with its subdivisions bluetick and English, is the least uniform; yet those who have had good ones stand steadfast in believing them the greatest of all cooners. A large number of hunters breed these two types and are sincerely striving toward uniformity. Examine any group of blueticks and see if you do not agree that, handsome though these dogs are, the type should not vary as much as it does.

In size alone the difference is tremendous. One outstanding breeder is striving for 100-pound hounds. Others think twenty-four-inch, fifty-five-pound dogs are large enough. Some are black and white, ticked; some are tricolored, ticked; and there are often red-and-white ticked pups from both types which owners feel should be registered. The ticking, as we saw in Chapter 4, is but a color modifier; and, unless we are mistaken, it is in no way correlated with treeing ability. Blue belton setters are distinguished by this factor, and certainly they are bird dogs, not tree dogs.

Even in the matter of voice there is no uniformity. The standard asks only for a hound voice. They may drawl, bugle, or chop on the trail.

One noted breeder has been attempting to make his hounds resemble bloodhounds, but tricolored and ticked. Another breeds for dogs as quick and lithe as dogs can be.

In coat many blueticks have longer hair than Red-bones or black-and-tans.

Bluetick breeders claim, rightly or wrongly, that their breeds excel in the mental quality of trueness for coons without running trash. Our own experience with blue-ticks has been unusually good. Many of our best dogs were of this type. Although there is considerable dif-ference among the dogs of the breed, the loveliest, sweetest, and most powerful hound voice we ever heard was that of Buck, an Arkansas bluetick, which weighed only fifty-five pounds.

Another excellent quality is the early starting which many blueticks display. The family cat often finds it necessary to take to a tree with four-months-old puppies after her.

Some of the highest prices ever paid for coonhounds have been paid for blueticks. The breed receives con-siderable publicity from being used by mountain-lion and bear hunters, and the stud fees that can be collected from such noted animals justify their high prices. Blue-tick owners are often ardent advertisers and have done more to popularize their breed than owners of other breeds.

BLUETICK COONHOUND STANDARD: OFFICIAL U.K.C.

The following men assisted in preparing this stan-dard: O. O. Grant, C. O. Smith, Ray Campbell, Bill Harshman, Carrol Suits, Daryl Hunter, F. G. Reeder, Elbett Vaughn, Thurman Houston, Dr. E. G. Fuhrman.

This standard has been framed for three real purposes:

1. To act as a guide for the U.K.C. and its judges at bench shows.

2. To furnish suggestions for breeders in their aims toward improving the breed, to higher ideals in their breeding.

3. To advance this breed to one of similar sameness throughout the country.

Head and Neck. Ears well attached slightly below top of skull, should be thin with slight roll, taper well toward a point, and should reach well toward end of nose. Ears set low enough on head and devoid of erectile power. Ear well attached to head to prevent hanging or backward tilt.

Head skull very slightly domed, and broad between ears, never narrow. Length for males from occiput to end of nose, 9 to 10 inches; females, 8 to 9 inches.

Eyes should be rather large, set wide apart at the stop; stop prominent; expression pleading; color, dark brown or black, not lighter than hazel. Lids of eyes should be firm and close, without excess third eyelid showing (no drooping).

Muzzle from stop to end of nose should be square, well proportioned in width with the skull, with depth and flews well covering the lower jaw.

Depth of 3 to 4½ inches.

Height at Shoulders. Slightly higher at shoulders than at hips, never lower at shoulders than at hips. Males: 23 to 26 inches at shoulders. Females: 21 to 24 inches at shoulders.

Body. Neck should rise free from shoulders, with slight taper, not carried too high or too low, not thick as shoulders; muscular and of moderate length.

Throat clean, with very small trace of dewlap (excess dewlap objectionable).

Shoulders clean, gradually sloped and muscular, not broad and protruding, but to appear as part of body, showing freedom of movement and strength.

Chest should show considerable depth, rather than excessive width, allowing plenty of lung space, fairly even with front of shoulders, extending well down to the elbow, in girth for males, 26 to 34 inches; females 23 to 30 inches.

Ribs should be well sprung with good depth and taper gradually to short ribs, resembling a curve in the chest, rather than a sunken drop-off between chest and stomach. Ribs should gather at the shoulders, sloping well with neck when head is held at alert.

Back should be moderately long and muscular, tapering up to a high gather at the shoulders, sloping well with neck when head is held at alert.

Loins broad, well muscled, and slightly arched. Back length in comparison with height.

Forelegs straight from the shoulder down to the feet, well boned and muscular, with a strong straight pastern. Forelegs should appear straight from either side or front view.

Feet round with well-arched toes (no upward trend of toe claw). Thick tough pads. When standing should appear as a ball rather than to spread.

Hips strong and well muscled, width slightly less than rib spring. Rump should taper slightly with width in proportion to hips.

Thighs of gradual taper with excess muscular development giving abundant propelling power. Breeching full and clean down to hock.

Hocks firm and moderately bent, not excessively bent (as cow hock). Hind legs to appear straight with the body when viewed from behind.

Tail attached slightly below the back line, well rooted and tapering to a moderate length as compared with length of the hound. Carried high with a forward curve as of half moon. Tail well coated (no flag), no rat tail.

Coat medium coarse and laying close to body, to appear smooth and glossy. Neither too rough or too short.

Weight. Males: 55 to 80 pounds. Females: 45 to 65 pounds.

Appearance. Appearance of the bluetick coonhound should be that of speedy, well-muscled individual, straight up of racy type, not chunky and clumsily built. Body should be neat, coat glossy; head carried well up, but not goose-necked. Eyes clear and keen. Tail carried gaily above back, not curled or dropped between legs. Feet round and well padded. A pleading hound expression, not wild or cowed acting. Active, ambitious, and speedy on trail.

Voice. The bluetick should be a free tonguer on trail, with medium bawl or bugle voice when striking and trailing, may change to a steady chop when running, with a steady coarse chop at tree.

Color. Preferred color of the bluetick is a dark blue thickly mottled body spotted by various-shaped black spots on back and ears and sides. Preference running to more blue than black on body. Head with black predominating, also ears, tan dots over eyes and on cheeks with a dark red ticking on feet and lower legs below body line. Red may be eliminated as to the desire of the breeder, as well as the head coloring and amount of black on body. The amount of blue ticking should control over the amount of white in the body coat. Off-colors not allowed.

Teeth. Even, neither under- nor overshot.

Breeding. Only recognized pedigree and U.K.C. registered bloodlines acceptable.

Points

Head		25
Skull	5	
Ears	5	
Eyes	5	
Muzzle	10	
Body		40
Neck	5	
Chest and Shoulders	15	
Back and Loins	15	
Coat	3	
Tail	2	
Running Gear		35
Forelegs	10	
Hips, Thighs, Hind Legs	15	
Feet	10	

ENGLISH FOX AND COONHOUND STANDARD: OFFICIAL U.K.C.

This standard has been framed for two real purposes:

1. To act as a guide for the U.K.C. and its judges at bench shows.

2. To furnish suggestions for breeders in their aims toward improving the breed to higher ideals in their breeding.

Head and Neck. Ears hung a little low, fine texture and soft feel, reach nearly to end of nose if drawn out, not flat and stiff or half cocked. Muzzle good length, stop nearly medium. Flews enough to look square. Large, open nostrils. Skull very slightly domed, wide, never narrow. Eyes large, set wide apart, dark, never pig-eyed or drooping.

Teeth. Even, neither under- nor overshot.

Height at Shoulders. Slightly higher at shoulders than at hips, never lower at shoulders than at hips. Males: 22 to 25 inches. Females: 21 to 24 inches.

Body. Deep broad chest, strong back, slightly arched. Not roached back. Thighs and shoulders up and muscled strong. Good barrel, plenty of lung room. A strong racy type body.

Feet and Legs. Forelegs good bone, straight, strong, set well apart. Feet, cat's paw, strong arched over toes, pads deep, set directly under legs. The nails should be strong, well padded, stifles stout, well down. Hocks just a little bent. Hind legs strong, showing drive, power, push. Never cow hocked.

Tail or Stern. Carried gay, set high, but not hooked over back. Just a little brush shown. Medium length. Not rat-tailed.

Coat. Hair, hard, medium length of good hound type for protection.

Voice. A good hound bawl.

Color. This hound may be officially any good hound color, coming in ticks, the tricolor, and the black saddle.

Points

Head	10
Neck	5
Shoulders	10
Chest and Ribs	10
Back and Loins	15
Hind Quarters	10
Elbows	5
Legs and Feet	20
Coat and Color	5
Stern	5
General Make-up	5
	100

The Plott Hound

Since Plott hounds are among the fewest in numbers of the coonhounds, it might be thought they are the least desirable. This is untrue. Good Plotts are excep-

tionally fine cooners. We have owned a few, seen many,
and talked with owners. Each is most enthusiastic about
his dogs' abilities. As is true in the case of every type,
many dogs closely approximating Plotts are called by
that name. (We have known a collie and pit-bulldog
cross passing for a Plott hound.) This is one reason why
it pays to buy registered dogs.

The Plott hound differs slightly from hounds of other
types. First of all, the dogs are brindled. Most are black-
and-tans with the tan showing brindling. If the black
saddle were not covering the hound's body, the whole
animal would be brindled, and some actually are.

The typical Plott has a keen tough look. Weights
vary. We have seen them as small as thirty-five pounds
and as large as seventy-five. Probably because breeders
have cared less for appearance and have selected primarily for hunting ability. Plotts now have a less uniform type than others; but after all, a coonhound is
owned principally for performance and only partly for
appearance. The Plott gives the performance in a masterful manner. His voice is clear and carries well. He
can trail where it is dry, but he works in water equally
as well as dogs of any other type. He has proven to be a
sticker. Plotts are easily trained too, starting early. All
these virtues are not found in every hound, but a high
percentage of them is present in this excellent cooner.

PLOTT HOUND STANDARD: OFFICIAL U.K.C.

This standard was framed for the purpose of fur-
nishing suggestions for breeding to the breeders, in

their aims toward improving the breed, to higher ideals in their breeding.

To try and establish a nation-wide breed of this particular hound strain of bloodlines to look alike and to have a universal conformation.

Head. Carried well up, dome moderately flat, moderate width between and above eyes. Ears set moderately high and of medium length, soft and no erectile power.

Eyes brown or hazel, prominent, no drooping eyelids. Muzzle moderate length not square.

Shoulders. Muscular and sloping to indicate speed and strength.

Chest. Deep, with adequate lung space.

Back. Slightly arched, well muscled, not roached.

Hips. Smooth, round, proportionately wide, flanks gracefully arched, muscular quarters and loins.

Tail or Stern. Moderately heavy, strong at root, tapering, rather long without brush, carried free, well up, saberlike.

Front Legs. Straight, smooth, forearm muscular. Straight at knees, perfectly in line with upper leg.

Hind Legs. Strong and muscular above hock, but graceful, slightly bent at hock, no cow hock, speedy shaped and graceful.

Feet. Round solid, cat foot, well padded and knuckled, set directly under leg.

Color and Coat. Smooth haired, fine, glossy, but thick enough for protection in cold wind or water. Brindle or brindle with black saddle. Some white on chest or feet permissible.

Voice. Open trailing, bawl and chop.

Height. Males: 22 to 25 inches at shoulder. Females: 21 to 24 inches at shoulder.

Weight. Males: 50 to 60 pounds. Females: 40 to 55 pounds.

Characteristics of This Breed. Active, fast, bright, confident, courageous, vicious fighters on game, super treeing instinct, take readily to water, alert, quick to learn, have great endurance and beauty.

Points

Head	15
Neck	5
Shoulders	10
Chest and Ribs	10

Back and Loins	15
Hind Quarters	10
Elbows	5
Legs and Feet	15
Coat and Color	5
Stern	5
General Make-up	5
	100

The Treeing Walker

A black-and-tan tree hound is said to have been among the original dogs to start the famous Walker strain. Perhaps this treeing aptitude occasionally crops out as a recessive to account for the treeing Walkers. At any rate, not a few purebred Walkers have given up fox hunting and taken to treeing squirrels by day and coons or possums by night. Naturally, they have been eliminated from the packs of which they were members.

In a great many litters of blueticked dogs, 25 per cent of the puppies have been unticked, resembling Walkers in color, at least. These dogs have treed naturally. We have owned them—dogs sold us as treeing Walkers, which we found had no kinship to real Walkers.

Our impression of the treeing Walker is that it represents an excellent type of hound, mostly white, and often among the finest of tree dogs; but it is the least distinctive of the coonhound types except for color. Many treeing Walkers look like the true Walker hound; others look like tricolored hounds of any of the other types. Breeders of treeing Walkers are striving to produce dogs of excellent style and uniformity and will succeed, provided their ideal is kept before the eyes of every breeder so that each man will not try to type his own strain.

Approved by the members of the National Treeing Walker Association at meeting June 30, 1946, at Logansport, Indiana; approved and accepted by the U.K.C., Inc. The Stud Books were opened July 10, 1945, record-

ing the Walker (Treeing) as a fully recognized breed of coon and big game hounds.

Head and Neck. Head carried well up, occipital bone prominent, plenty of width between and above the eyes, flat rather than dome shaped, not mullet or chuckle headed.

Ears of medium length, set medium low, should hang

gracefully, inside part tipping toward muzzle, should not be too pointed at tip, slightly round or oval, soft and velvety, hanging in a roll when head is raised.

Eyes prominent, expressive, open, dark in color, never yellow or pale, no drooping eyelids or deep-set pig eyes.

Muzzle medium square, rather than long, slightly tapering, with flews sufficient to give a rather square appearance, stop not too prominent, or too abrupt. The line of the head and muzzle should not slope down from the parallel line of skull giving a Roman nose appearance, or sloped up giving a dish-faced appearance.

Nostrils rather large, prominent and black; lemon, liver, and pale nose not acceptable; a slightly sloping nostril not objectionable as long as it does not give the dog a snipy appearance.

Neck not too thick or too long, graceful and strong, free from dewlap.

Shoulders. Muscular, sloping, for strength and speed.

Chest. Moderately wide and deep, showing large lung and heart capacity.

Back. Rather short, gracefully arched, muscular, strong.

Hips. Round, smooth, proportionately wide and muscular, giving a racy, streamlined appearance.

Flanks well-arched, muscular quarters and loins.

Tail strong at root, tapering thin, moderately long, without flag, carried free, well up, saberlike.

Legs—Front. Straight, smooth, and muscular, forearm straight at knee and perfectly in line with upper leg, not pigeon-toed or out-toed.

Legs—Hind. Muscular and strong above hocks, slightly bent at hocks, speedily shaped, not cow hocked.

Feet. Round, solid, and direct under the legs, well padded, giving a catlike appearance.

Color and Coat. White predominating, with black and tan spots. Any other color combination may be penalized at the discretion of the judge, but not barred, such as white with black spots, not tan—white, black, and tan with black or tan predominating, or with some scattered ticking; no liver, lemon, brindle or bluish mottled markings permissible. Coat smooth haired, glossy, fine, yet dense enough for protection.

Voice. Preferably a clear ringing bugle voice on cold trail, changing to chop or turkey mouth on running trail, a deep throaty loud chop mouth at tree.

Height. Slightly more at shoulders than at hips. Shoulders should measure: Males: 23 to 26 inches. Females: 21 to 24 inches.

Weight. Males in show flesh should weigh 50 to 75 pounds. Females: 40 to 65 pounds.

Working dogs when shown will not be penalized when slightly under.

Qualitative Characteristics. Energetic, bright, intelligent, active, quick, fast, courageous, composed, confident, fearless, pleasant, kind, graceful, ambitious, speedy, with a superabundance of sense, endurance, training, hunting and treeing instinct and ability.

Hound Crosses

Let no one sneer at the mention of the mongrel coonhound or coon dog. There are thousands which give their owners as much fun in hunting and field trials as any hound of any breed or type. We have owned them. One of us feels that the greatest coon getter he ever owned was a Redbone; the other believes his best was a Redbone and farm shepherd cross.

Ask any oldtimer and you may learn that he thinks a hound cross is best, perhaps one of the following: a springer spaniel and bloodhound, a beagle and collie, a bulldog and Airedale, or a shepherd and pointer. He will usually say that it was a cross which made a good still trailer, but you may find it was the only coon dog he ever owned and that he had no really top cooner with which to compare his mongrel.

Even annual records of coon pelts taken are not a fair gauge of a dog's quality as a cooner. Some men hunt every good night and run up large catches with inferior dogs. Others haven't that much time to spend and are content to get a few coons with a truly reliable hound. It is only when a hunter has owned many top cooners and is an avid hunter that he can judge the quality of a real coon dog.

A few general principles in breed crossing to produce coon dogs are interesting and valuable to know. Since, as we have seen, the open-trailing aptitude is dominant over the still trailing, the quality of the yapping voice is dominant over the beautiful hound quality, and the poorer scenting ability of a nonhound is dominant over a hound's keenness of scent, then the product of crossing a fine hound with a nonhound is an open trailer with a yappy voice and without a very keen nose— usually not much better than the nonhound.

An exception to this last trait occurs when the non-hound is a bird dog, but in that case another factor enters the picture. The bird dog tends to hunt with his head up and to quarter instead of getting down and trailing. This quality is decidedly dominant over the hound trailing. The crossing of a hound and bird dog, therefore, results in a dog of questionable value—a good air scenter but an inferior trailer. Springer spaniels, which are fair trailers, are exceptions among the bird dogs. In crosses with hounds they often produce excellent coon dogs.

Here are some crosses which were not successful, contrary to expectation:

> Irish setter and bloodhound
> Pointer and bloodhound
> English setter and foxhound
> Pointer and foxhound

We have seen dogs from these crosses which would try terribly hard to trail; but their innate propensities, or what psychologists call *behavior patterns,* wouldn't let them.

Old-fashioned farm shepherds were our first coon dogs, and in crosses with hounds their short-haired offspring (the long hair being recessive) frequently have speed, zest, and great endurance, together with a piercing quality of voice which can be heard a long distance, even though the voice lacks the quality of the hound's.

Hound mongrels often possess a determination to get the coon with but little interest in the trail itself. They take short cuts. With them it's the coon that counts. You see them quit a trail and rush around hunting for a fresher place, and thus they keep ahead of the pure hounds. Often they are good only when scenting conditions are prime, on damp drizzly nights or when there is a heavy dew. On dry nights it is often just as well to stay home as to try to hunt with one.

All of this is speaking in generalities. There are exceptions, to be sure; but, if any reader is planning to cross breeds to obtain a better hunter, these facts should be taken into consideration.

In buying such a dog, get the owner to demonstrate on a dry night, unless you don't mind hunting only on the few choice nights of the year. You can usually depend on the dog's being a good hunter if he has been properly trained. He may work hard to find trails fresh enough to follow, and when he finds them he won't have to trail for long because he will be so close to the coon. He may also be a far ranger, perhaps too far.

For field-trial work, the hound cross often excels. Some of the best have been just such dogs. Good noses are unnecessary. Any cur can usually follow the spoor of a bag of wet coon dung and urine. Hound crossing has been done many times to produce good field-trial dogs. Even Doberman pinschers, German shepherds, and greyhounds have been used—all breeds sorely lacking in scenting ability; but who besides the true hound lover cares? What most field-trial enthusiasts want is to win.

6. *The Still Trailer*

THE IDEAL CALLS for only one type of dog, whereas all coon hunters know that mongrels have often proved very expert at coon hunting.

Probably millions of words have been published on the question of whether the still trailer or the open trailer is the better hound for getting game. We have owned many of both kinds, and our opinion is that the dog which is a perfect hound in type and also a still trailer as far as voice is concerned will get more coons than any other kind. This combination—still-trailing pure hound—will get more coons than will the open trailer. Very few of the still trailers, however, have as good noses, coupled with the hunting aptitude, as has the pure hound; and this generally accounts for the fact that still trailers get fewer coons in a season.

The man who is more interested in enjoying the sport of coon hunting than in bringing home a great many coons should select an open trailer as his hunting dog. The open trailer gives his quarry warning and allows him a better chance to escape, and the hunter gets vastly more sport in this manner.

Right here we must bring out a point which is so often overlooked by coon hunters. We have heard comments along the following lines time after time; and, because nearly all coon hunters seem to hold this opinion, we feel we must set them straight so far as we are able. As a good illustration:

A party of hunters has gone off into the woods and come to a place where there is a good chance of getting a coon. They sit down, and the dog goes off ranging. They sit for perhaps ten or fifteen minutes, and suddenly someone hears the dog's voice far off in the distance.

"There he goes," he says. Perhaps for a minute nothing more than one sharp bark will be heard, then another minute or two of stillness. Finally the barking comes steadily from the throat of the dog. Another hunter says, "Got him straight, now." And soon another will remark, "My, but that coon can run." The dog may lead on for ten or fifteen minutes or more, and the members of the party will remark one after another about what an awful runner that raccoon is.

As a matter of fact, the raccoon is probably not running at all. The dog is doing all the running. The idea that the raccoon is dodging around, climbing up one tree and coming down another is, for the most part, unfounded. Let us, therefore, describe the probable actions of a raccoon which is being followed by a dog and see how different they really are from what the hunter thinks.

The raccoon has come out of his den around six-thirty, sometimes five-thirty, depending on the season of the year. He has probably waddled down to a brook, taking his time. He may have walked along the edge of the brook, sipping water now and again and looking for fish or a frog which has belatedly lingered on top of the mud before hibernating for the winter. Then, maybe he remembers a sweet apple tree on the other side of a hill. He ambles over to that, scratching here and there in the leaves, picking up grubs and looking for field mice as he goes. Finally he arrives at the tree and chews on a few apples. Then he remembers a place where there were beechnuts on his last visit. To it he goes and fills his paunch with beechnuts, walking from one tree to another and never doing a very thorough job on the ground beneath each one. He may stop and eat some acorns. By eleven-thirty he has wandered perhaps a total of two and a half miles.

By eleven o'clock the coon hunters have come into the woods near the place where he started. His track has been an extremely zigzagging one. He may have walked up a fallen log and climbed down off the other end just to satisfy his curiosity. He may have climbed up a den tree, looked into a hole, climbed out on a limb, and gone down again. He may have done the things that only a raccoon would naturally do. The dog picks up the trail, let us say, near the starting point and pursues this track. At first the track is somewhat old; but, as he goes along, the scent becomes stronger.

Now the coon hears the dog's voice in the distance, but he has heard hundreds of other dogs in the distance and pays no attention to it. He goes about his business, eating and exhibiting his curiosity at every turn. He cocks an ear and listens to the dog. He notices that the dog's voice is now nearer than it was. He is all attention for a little while, and then he starts to amble away. He does not run but just walks along at an easy gait in the opposite direction from the dog. He notices that the dog is getting closer and closer; so he hastens toward a big tree a few hundred yards away. Toward the end of the journey he may be running at a fairly good clip. Generally, however, he never runs more than fifty to a hundred yards and quite often he picks out the biggest tree he can find in the woods. Up he goes and sits there, because that is his chief method of defending himself. He doesn't go very high in the tree—only high enough to be out of harm's way—and waits for the dog to go by. However, the dog does not go by but comes to the foot of the tree and barks. The raccoon climbs higher in the tree.

All the while that the dog is following the trail, the hunters have the mistaken idea that he is hot on the coon's tail and that the coon is evading the dog by making all sorts of fancy curves, putting every obstacle in his way. Those who know raccoons know that they do no such thing, despite all the word to the contrary. Of course, the longer the trail has been, the greater the honor to the dog for having "outwitted" this crafty raccoon. A certain amount of honor does belong to the dog, not for outwitting the raccoon but simply for following a crooked and troublesome trail and having the perseverance to follow it, stay at the foot of the tree, and bark until the hunters get there. Piecing together the likely behavior of the raccoon from what we have been able to study about the natural habits of the animal, that is just about what happens in an average coon hunt. There are exceptions. Some coons will run like foxes for hours, but we're talking about the average coon.

Knowing this, one has a better idea of the relative merits of the still trailer and the open trailer. The still trailer picks up the trail and follows it. The coon doesn't get a chance to hear the barking of the dog in the distance, the first thing he knows, a tornado comes dashing through the woods at him, and he takes refuge in the first bush or tree at hand. Sometimes he will even tree on a corn shock, hide in a brush pile, or jump into the water if any is nearby. Of course, the still trailer can do this. He can also hunt coons with greater assurance of success in ledgy country, because a coon which has been reared in the ledges is more apt to run to them for protection than he is to climb a tree. When he hears the voice of an approaching hound, if he is where he can make it, he will dash for a ledge and be safe. A still trailer, however, will run up on the coon before he knows what he is about, and he will have to tree in the first thing at hand.

We must remember that many raccoons are killed by still trailers in open lots and allowed to lie there and decay. We must also remember that the still trailer becomes lost on many occasions. Suppose, for example, that you are on one side of a hill and the wind comes up. The dog starts on a long tedious trail and eventually winds up barking tree two miles away. This is no idle dream—it often happens. Then, because of the wind, the hunters are unable to hear the dog and he has to stay there, sometimes all night, barking tree if he has the perseverance to stay that long. This is cruelty. Besides, it is nerve-racking to the hunter and requires a great deal of extra walking to find the dog. We feel that we could write a book on the merits of hunting with a still versus an open trailer, but we believe that it is sufficient to sum up the discussion by saying that hunting with a still trailer is poor sport as compared with using an open trailer—hearing the stirring voice, understanding the direction the coon has taken and the ways in which he has waddled about the woods, learning something about his natural habits, and having a full evening's enjoyment by hunting with a beautiful-voiced open trailer. What greater thrill can a hunter experience than hearing those notes ring over hill and valley, ending with the different tone of voice calling the hunter to come, come, come!

However, much the sporting angle appeals, and it does to most hunters, there will still be those who want to own and breed still trailers. We know of instances where no one can blame them. In those states like the Traprock State—Connecticut—catching coons with open trailers is often most difficult because the coons soon become trained to crawl into the nearest ledge. These hillsides of tumble-down, angular rocks afford perfect protection. There a hunter is fortunate indeed to have his open trailers tree a third of the coons they start.

What crosses or purebreds make the best still trailers? Usually those which are not too remote from hounds. Fighting bulldogs, bull terriers, farm shepherds, Dalmatians, Airedales, springer spaniels, retrievers of all breeds—these have made still trailers. Crosses between them have produced some outstanding coon getters.

If any hunter has such crosses in mind, he can refer to the chart on page 36 and see what to expect. If the dogs used are pure, he will find that the result will pretty much follow the prediction.

The worst feature of breed crosses is that they are one-generation affairs—exceedingly unstable. You may get a star, but his or her pups will tend to be diverse and will be far less likely to duplicate the parent than will the pups of purebred parents.

7. *How to Obtain a Coon Dog*

THE QUESTION is always arising, "Shall I breed my own
dogs or shall I buy them?" Since so many hunters have
no facilities for raising puppies and must be content
with one or two dogs, for them buying dogs is in order.
Most experienced hunters have, besides their mainstay,
another puppy coming along; so we shall have to consider two problems:

1. How to obtain a puppy.
2. How to obtain a trained dog.

In Chapter 5 we have outlined the salient points of each of the breeds of cooners, and in Chapter 6 we have discussed the still trailer. These chapters give you a fairly good idea of the available types; now you decide what you want, and, having decided, you read advertisements.

There are in the United States, as this is written, several excellent magazines, each of which will stimulate any coon hunter's spirits and ambitions; and we suggest you subscribe to one or more. Here they are, with a few notes about each:

Full Cry, Sedalia, Missouri, published for "the American coonhound and treehound enthusiasts." Big-game hound news is also included. This illustrated magazine is the largest in form and circulation, going to about 15,000 hunters and field-trial men and used by the largest number for advertising. Well illustrated and earthy, it talks the hunter's language. Here, besides coon dogs for sale, you will find field trials advertised and reports of the results.

The American Cooner, Wickliff, Kentucky. A magazine catering only to coon hunters and coonhound field-trial enthusiasts and edited from their point of view. It reports field-trial results and advertises them in advance. Many pictures.

Mountain Music, 110 Sixth St., Monroe, Louisiana, is also a coon hunters' journal. It reports field trials, show results, and contains interesting matter written by coon hunters for coon hunters. *Mountain Music* is also well illustrated and advertisements are generally large-scale.

Bloodlines, the official organ of the United Kennel Club, the organization registering most of our coonhound breeds, is published by that organization from Hanselman Building, Kalamazoo, Michigan. It usually contains comments on coonhounds and several pages of advertisements.

Redbone Trailhound News, 2525 East York St., Philadelphia 25, Pennsylvania, is the only breed publication among the several breeds. It comes at present in mimeographed form and contains some advertisements, along with news and comments of the Redbone fraternity members.

Besides these magazines especially for coon hunters, there are many others carrying advertisements of coon dogs. All of the great outdoor magazines and many magazines such as *The Chase, Red Ranger,* and others related, which cater to hound lovers of all kinds, carry coonhound advertising. *Field & Stream* offers an editorial service to assist buyers in procuring the dogs they desire from reliable sources. Another source is the farm magazines, each of which carries a column of dog advertisements.

Our preference is for *Full Cry, The American Cooner,* and *Mountain Music,* when we look for puppies to buy, because the small kennels that raise choice pups from dogs they hunt and know do not need the vast circulation of the general magazines to sell their puppies. The advertising rates also are low enough for a man to be able to describe his pups better, and you know without too much correspondence what to expect. Such detailed advertisements save your time.

It is always better to go personally and select the puppy. If you go, you may see the parents, not having to take the owner's word about their appearance. The puppies can, in a general way, be expected to look like them and inherit the same behavior patterns. If you can't travel for a personal examination, you must write.

Don't be afraid to pay a good price for a puppy. We know many hunters who have regretted being penny wise and dollar foolish. They have bought $10 puppies and have spent $200 raising them to a year on fancy meat diets, only to realize they picked lemons. How much better to have spent $50 for a royally bred puppy and perhaps $30 for good dog food for the year and to have a dog to be proud of at the end!

Which brings us to the economics of whether it pays to raise your own puppies. For sentimental reasons there is no argument; it pays. Economically it is a waste. You can buy a well-started, full-grown puppy almost any time for less than the cost of buying a very young puppy and raising him. Using the better grades of dry meal-type dog foods and up to 25 per cent of edible fat with it, it costs, at today's prices, at least $30 to raise a puppy for ten months. Even by using home-mixed formulas, it costs nearly as much. Table scraps are useful, but they cost money too, a fact most people forget. When there is a dog in the home, Mother usually, perhaps unconsciously, buys a little more of everything so there will be scraps. They cost much more than good meal-type dog food.

Coonhounds raised strictly on a canned-food diet cost more than $150 to raise for ten months, and it is necessary to use the best canned foods or puppies may grow up with several kinds of deficiencies.

One amusing fact about puppy sales is the seasonal demand. Hunters become "steamed up" with enthusiasm during the hunting season and buy puppies at that time, not thinking of the long years ahead before the pup becomes an expert. One would think they expected the baby pup to start treeing as soon as it arrived. Beagle breeders also often remark that it is so easy to sell beagle puppies during the hunting season and difficult during the rest of the year.

This should not be. The wise hunter is not mindful of his requirements during hunting season only; he thinks ahead and plans. The knowledge that the great majority of inexperienced hunters buy up the puppies during hunting season makes him realize he can get a better selection and a better buy in spring, say, when the breeders are having difficulty unloading their pups.

Buying a trained dog is another matter. We have already discussed the magazines in which advertisements appear. The main question is, *how far can these ads be trusted?* Other considerations are: Shall you buy from a dog dealer or an individual? Shall you buy by mail? Shall you go personally and see the dog you buy? How much should you pay? Does a guarantee mean anything?

How long a guarantee should you require? What is a fair guarantee? What is a fair trial period?

The authors have sold dogs and have seen the results. Here are some examples of what can happen.

A grand black-and-tan hound, which, the previous season, had treed forty-five coons, was sold in good faith to an inexperienced coon hunter. The dog had no bad habits and was full of hunt. For some reason, one night during the trial he ran a fox a short way and quit. The neophyte, not knowing it was a fox he'd run, took him back and urged him to continue. He did and turned into an excellent foxhound. His value dropped 60 per cent.

Another example is that of an outstanding cooner sold to a man addicted to *spiritus frumenti*—liquor, in our language—who took the dog hunting. The dog, a two-and-a-half-year-old hound, treed in a swamp. The hunter was too drunk to wade out and get the dog. He barked for several hours. The hunter went home. It began to rain. When the dog was found the next day, he was sick. Before he could die, the buyer returned him to the seller, and the dog was dead upon arrival. There are persons like that, believe it or not.

A third example is a seven-year-old homesick dog, one which had treed several hundred coons. He was sold to a first-class hunter who tried him for a week. The dog refused to leave the lantern light. This hunter believed the seller and personally took the dog back. That night seller and buyer went hunting. The dog ranged for half-hour spells, treed two coons, and was taken back by the buyer who, by using patience, gained his new pal's confidence and owned a truly great cooner.

Every year sellers ship hundreds of oustanding coonhounds which are returned because of some minor fault such as a few barks at a rabbit, being underweight, chasing a deer for a hundred yards, failing to stay treed long enough, failing to follow a drag made from a bag of coon dung, failing to jump into a lake and follow a coon, or showing timidity about killing a coon. Not one of these faults should be the basis for returning a dog, because each can be corrected with patience.

Dog sellers know what they are up against. When a dog is returned, out he goes again to another buyer and after a few trials, somebody is likely to have the dog run across a hot trail, tree a small coon, kill it, and convince the buyer that he owns the best coon dog in the U.S.A.

But from the buyer's point of view, we must acknowledge that he gets some shellacking—to use the colloquial term. One year we sent to eight sellers for a dog and returned seven. Each had all kinds of chances to make good. Four of the seven were deer dogs par excellence. One was a foxhound. One wouldn't tree, and the last wouldn't leave the lantern—he was afraid of the dark. These were all expensive dogs. The one we kept was a poor underfed, overworked creature with cankered ears and hookworm, whipworm, and tapeworm infestation. But what a tree dog! All of those minor ailments were quickly treated.

There are shippers, completely unscrupulous, who

buy good-looking but unsatisfactory dogs and keep shipping them on short trials until they get lost or run over
or overstay the trial period. They take little risk. There
are others who send out price lists based on double the
express charges from them to you. Naturally you won't
want to bother with returning one. These are cheap
dogs for "suckers." Best not to patronize such kennels.

Another kind of seller to watch for is the one who
advertises one dog in many magazines. A man with one
fine hound knows that one small advertisement will sell it.
He doesn't need to run ads in several outdoor magazines
to sell "Mike, the greatest cooner in Kentucky—caught
thirty coons last season," etc. His record will sell him.
The only reason for advertising such a dog at all is to
get him out of the county on account of competition or
to receive more money from a long-distance buyer. What
such an ad means is that Mike is perhaps a hundred
dogs; the one advertisement is the extent of the dealer's
seasonal efforts.

What kind of dog can you expect to buy from a
dealer? Only as good a dog as the dealer can buy from
hunters. Once in a while any dealer will get hold of
a *real* dog. Perhaps some hunter's wife owes a payment
on the washing machine; money is needed to keep
Junior in college; the telephone will be taken out if the
bill isn't paid. It means, "Sell old Rock; we've got some
good pups coming along." But dealers pick up very few
dogs of that quality. What they get are dogs with just
enough faults that the owner doesn't want them and is
willing to sell. These are the rejects. Often such dogs

in the hands of understanding and patient hunters can be cured of their objectionable habits.

Put yourself in the position of a hunter with three or four hounds. Here comes the dog buyer. He wants dogs. Do you sell him your best? It is no exaggeration to say that there are hundreds of hunters whose dogs have afforded them so much more undiluted pleasure than their wives that they would not hesitate to give up a wife before they would part with their old hounds. That's true. So don't expect to buy their dogs from dealers. Not that you could get their wives either, but you probably wouldn't want one of the type they'd be willing to part with.

The dealer often has scouts who comb the countryside and keep him posted on the hounds up for sale. He may not have a single dog on the premises if you call on him, but the expressman will tell you he ships out three or four a day during the height of the season. Those dogs are each taken from the hunter directly to the depot. The dealer is busy answering correspondence and building crates.

In buying a hound at a distance, two important facts should be borne in mind. Buy one acclimated, and buy one from country where there is game of the same kind you have at home. To amplify:

If you are a northern Wisconsin hunter, don't buy an Alabama hound, with his short sparse coat, and expect him not to feel the cold the first season. Such a hound the next season will have become acclimated. In short, buy dogs accustomed to the same general cli-

mate as that in which you live and hunt. We have had
Alabama and Mississippi hounds come to Michigan and
Connecticut, where we live, and hunt the first season,
but all of them did a lot of shivering.

If you live in a porcupine-infested country, try to
buy a northern dog you won't have to break from running them. If you don't, you may have but one short
hunt—the first—all season.

If you live in a deer-infested state, don't buy a dog
from Kansas, for example, expecting the dog not to
touch deer, because almost every spirited cooner we've
ever seen will run deer unless trained not to. Buy a dog
from a place where deer abound.

The ideal way to buy a dog is to go and watch the
dog work. If you think the seller is an unscrupulous
person who has let a coon out and left it in a tree with
someone keeping it there until the dog arrives, expecting you to be satisfied with one short hunt, have him
bring the dog to you, and you take dog and owner into
territory where there is everything but coons. If the dog
hunts but doesn't start anything, *then* take him where
there are coons. Such a trial is worth something.

Buying a dog on trial may be satisfactory, provided
the trial is long enough. Six-day trial periods are a joke.
Shipping alone can take six days, three each way. At
least demand that the dog shall be *in your hands* for
six days; disdain any trial period which includes the
time on the road—you are not trying the dog while the
shipping agency has him.

There are tricks aplenty which dog dealers know.

They may ship you several dogs, one after the other, until your expressage has eaten up your equity. Then they may tell you they have three dogs culled from all the dogs they have bought that year which they keep for their own personal hunting. This is said in an off-hand manner. If you rise to the bait, you may have to pay many hundreds of dollars for such a dog—and even then it may be no better than some you've returned.

In regard to the guarantee, the seller is protected in many ways. First, he gets your money. You'll get it back all right because Uncle Sam watches the mails. Or he may have you deposit it in a bank or with the Railway Express Agency, an airline, or a motor-trucking line. It is safer from your point of view to have the money at your end, because if a dog is an obvious dud and you can prove it, you can attach the money and make the dealer fight for it. He knows it will cost him more to get it than it will to send you a good dog. If he keeps it and the Postal Inspector, after examining the correspondence, finds he has lived up to his claims, which often are so vague they are meaningless, then you will have to fight.

How this works is as follows: You buy a dog with the understanding that he is deer-proof. Your letter says not to send a dog that will run deer. The first time you and several reputable witnesses take him hunting, he starts a deer and you never see him again. Let's say the deer runs right past you; you see him with your flashlights. But you never see the dog again. You can't return the dog. In that case, you can't win.

The hazards of buying dogs by mail are great indeed, made even greater by high transportation rates. To ship any medium-sized dog halfway across the United States costs at least $18. The crate must be figured in on the weight, and the combined weight of the crate and the dog is once and a half the ordinary first-class express rate.

Try to minimize these hazards by considering the suggestions in this chapter. They are based on expensive personal experience.

8. *Training the Coon Dog*

IF THE READER will recall the qualifications mentioned in the preceding chapters, he will realize that the first and foremost requirement of the coon dog is that he have certain natural aptitudes. Let us, then, start with a dog which we are convinced has these aptitudes.

How are we going to train him? A good many methods have been suggested, but the one which has been used by the authors to the best effect will be described first. We shall, of course, assume that there is no other dog with whom he can be trained. Let us suppose that the dog starts out as a rank amateur but with the proper potentialities. Then, we are going to train him to range out wide, to find only coon tracks or tracks of animals that live in trees, to follow these tracks until the animal climbs a tree, and to sit at the foot of the tree and bark until we arrive there, showing him our appreciation for his splendid efforts and catching the animal either alive or dead. How shall we go about it?

The first thing we must do is get the dog, somehow, to understand what we want him to do. As each step is properly performed by the dog, we must get across to him in any way we can the fact that we are pleased. It isn't necessary to reward him with food; appreciation will be all the satisfaction and reward he will want. A good friendly thumping on the side with the open hand will repay him ten times more than Hamburg steak. "Well done, good and faithful servant" is the thought that you must communicate to him. He doesn't want to be rewarded; he simply wants to serve you.

"The greatest firmness is the greatest mercy," and these words apply especially to dog training. You must be absolutely firm at all times with the dog. Never start anything that you can't finish; never allow a single slip to occur, or it will undo a great deal of the good you have already done.

First teach the dog some rudimentary words. Get him to understand the meaning of a few phrases and always be sure to use the same words for the same thing.

"Good boy" is the most important idea to convey to

the dog. The second most important is "Don't touch." No one needs to be taught how to make his dog understand what the first one means, but it is not always easy for the novice to understand how to get the latter meaning across. We do it in this way: Take the dog into a room where he can't run away, throw a large piece of meat on the floor in front of him, and say, "Don't touch." He will touch it, of course, because the words mean nothing to him. As he does so, slap his face very hard. Throw the meat down again and say, "Don't touch." If he tries it again, you must slap him again; but if he is an intelligent dog, usually this is nearly enough.

Then teach him what "Take it" means. Cut a little piece of the meat off and throw it down to him and say, "Take it," patting him if he does. Having accomplished this, you are ready to go farther. Try stepping around the corner and throwing the meat into the room where the dog is and saying, "Don't touch," from a distance. When you are sure that he knows exactly what you mean and also knows what you mean by "Take it," you are ready to drag a piece of meat.

Get a bag of old stale meat and drag it along the ground, going by the corner of a building. Hide yourself behind the corner and let someone liberate the dog and show him the trail. He will at once start to trail the meat. If he has gone by where you are standing, just call, "Don't touch." If he continues to follow it, run after him and make him quit. In this way, you will be able to control his running on the trail of an animal just as you do on the trail of the meat. When the dog thoroughly understands this lesson, it is time to take him out into the woods.

Secure for yourself a captive raccoon, one that will lead comfortably. A tame raccoon that can be harnessed will be best of all.

Lead your coon around on a trail at least half a mile long. Let him climb a small tree but be up sufficiently high that he will be out of reach of the dog. After letting the dog exercise, take him to where the trail has been started and let him trail it. The dog will run to the tree, see the coon, and stand there barking excitedly. Run to the dog and pet him for all you are worth. Show him how much you appreciate what he has done.

The next night, if possible, repeat the procedure, but put the coon a little higher in the tree. The third, fourth, or fifth night thereafter, lead the coon around and put him up in a very high tree, so far up that the dog cannot see him. Have a woodchuck tied up in the tree also in a burlap sack or box of some sort. When the dog has treed the coon, go to him, pet him, and then climb the tree. Shoot the woodchuck and throw him out. When the woodchuck hits the ground, the dog will "kill it"; your partner on the ground should encourage him in this. There is something about this "killing" that seems to make the dog much more ravenous for hunting.

A number of training methods have been advocated by hunters which involve using live raccoons and allowing the dog to fight or kill them. Some of these recommendations have won prizes in magazine contests for the best method. One man related leading a coon just ahead of a dog who was held back by his handler and prevented from inflicting too much damage on the coon. The coon naturally ran and yet was not given his freedom. At the foot of a tree, a fight was permitted, and then the coon was allowed to climb the tree, exciting the dog to frantic barking. The coon was held by a light chain just out of reach of the dog and, after enough excitement, was thrown out for the dog to kill.

This brutality is completely unnecessary and degrading to the trainers. The method, however, is meritorious; it can be fully as effective if the dog is not permitted to touch the coon and if, in the end, the coon is shot in the brain and then thrown out. The dog doesn't know he didn't kill the coon.

Remember that some of the best tree dogs of all time have not been vicious killers; they love to trail and bay on the trail. When the trail goes up a tree they, being unable to climb, simply stand at the foot and continue to bay, encouraged to do so by the knowledge that the baying brings the hunter. Many a great hound has been perfectly content to stand back and let his hunter bag the game when it fell from the tree. The majority, however, seem to love the fight—especially the one-sided fight of themselves against a wounded or dying coon.

When two or more hounds are hunted together, the reaction is almost always altered by jealousy. No dog, in our experience, has been willing to stand back and not attack when another tackles a coon. The dog which may be perfectly willing to let you bag a coon without interference from himself will, if another dog interferes, take hold too. In fact, each may try to take the coon away from the other and drag it off into the woods.

Now that the dog has learned to tree you are ready to teach him to range. This is most easily done by letting him know what you mean when you say, "Find him." Say this when you start him on the trail each time. Then gradually let him go farther and farther from the trail so that he has to do some hunting to find the beginning of it. After you have gotten him to range off a hundred yards hunting for that trail which he has come to know is surely there, take him as much as a quarter of a mile away from it, and finally half a mile. Of course, he will often run onto the track close to the tree, but this will do no harm. As he becomes more and more experienced, you will find that you can take him where there are coons and simply say, "Find him," and then it will seem to the dog as though he were being taken near the specially laid trail. He will range off trying to find a trail. When he has become conscious that he has a job to do and that it is all part of a partnership between you and him, it will not hurt him at all if occasionally you go out and find no coon tracks. He will search just as diligently.

You must obtain a permit to train the dog in some states.

If you live in the South, you will find that your dog often trees possums, but this will be very useful to him. If you live in the North, he will tree porcupines. You must then carry pincers with you and be ready to remove hundreds of quills after the dog has munched on his first porcupine.

In the daytime it is often very valuable to take the dog squirrel hunting. Let him know that he has pleased you just as much as though he had treed a coon. This is a safe practice because squirrels are seldom out at night, except occasionally when there is bright moonlight.

Do not think that you can make a great coon dog by sitting home reading or by thinking how it should be done and imagining that you are working on the dog. That is the chief way many owners "train" their dogs and the reason most coon dogs are so poorly trained. To make a real trailer of your dog, you must work hard and long until you have made him understand that going out in the evening with you is equivalent to going on a coon hunt. When he is well trained, he will get so excited at the sight and smell of your old hunting clothes, your flashlight, and gun or revolver that he will forget all about supper, comfort, and anything else.

You are now ready for the real part of training. We shall assume that you have taught the dog to range well. Now it behooves you to teach him to trail only tree-living animals. Without doubt, if you are a hunter, you know your country. You know the deer runs, and some of the fox runs. Rabbits, you realize, run in small circles, unless they are a large variety, in which case they run in circles about a mile in diameter.

Your dog is accustomed to being petted and to hearing the words, "Good boy." It will come as a great shock to him to hear you saying something else. Don't be afraid of straining your voice by yelling at him, "Don't touch," when you realize that he is on the wrong trail. Don't be afraid to scold him. He's the only companion that won't kick at cuss words, and having used them on the dog will make you better natured at home.

Breaking from Rabbits

As soon as you hear your dog make one or two small circles, you may be reasonably sure he is chasing rabbits. Go quietly to the place where the rabbit has run and sit there. When the rabbit comes around again, get ready, a stout switch in your hand. The rabbit will dodge you, but you will very likely hear him. As soon as the dog comes along, jump out and catch him by the collar, holding him by the back of the neck, and thrash him until it hurts. Scold him and show him by your every action how terribly disappointed you are in him.

Since he may not have understood your punishment, give him a chance to show you. Attach a strong twenty-foot cord to his collar and let him go. If he goes back to the rabbit's track again, pull him up short, larrup him some more, and scold a great deal. Repeat, and the third time he probably won't go back, for he has learned that "Don't touch" applies to rabbits.

Actually, breaking the dog from running rabbits is the simplest thing you have to do.

Breaking from Fox and Deer

The best method we know for breaking from fox and deer is hunting the dog in the daytime. We prefer to train when we can see what is happening. The dog can see at night, and hunting after dark when he has been used to daylight hunting is a simple transition.

If you live where there is snow part of the year, it is a simple matter to break the dog from fox and deer. As soon as he shows the slightest interest in running a trail out in the open where there is no likelihood of squirrels having been, get to him and thrash him. You can tell from the track what the game is. If there is no snow, you can judge pretty well what character of game it most likely was. You can also tell from the attitude of the dog. A yell from you—"Don't touch"—will usually bring him cringing on his belly toward you.

At night it is difficult to distinguish the running raccoon from the running fox unless they can be heard. The latter runs very quietly, taking long hops, while the raccoon turns the leaves under foot and makes much more noise. The rabbit seems to be mostly up in the air, coming to earth long enough to make another mighty hop; you can hear the jumps at intervals. The deer, on the other hand, comes thrashing through the brush, interested in getting away. It is almost always easy to distinguish the deer, provided you are near enough to hear the animal at all. If you will keep your lights out, you will more often than not be able to hear.

There have been many plans suggested for training dogs to let deer alone. Some tie a gland from the back leg of a deer to the dog's collar and allow it to rot. The smell is said to make the dog forever sick of deer, but we know cases when this did not work.

The best way to break your dog from deer will be to take him into country where there are many crossroads. Take a light twenty-foot rope with you—one with a swivel snap in one end. Have your dog's collar tight. Drive out with three companions, if possible, as though you were going coon hunting, liberate the dog where you know deer are likely to be, and get back to the car while the dog is ranging. As soon as he starts the deer, listen carefully for his direction. Deer generally run on paths which go fairly straight, seldom going in circles as foxes and rabbits do. Drive as fast as you can for a crossroad which will probably intercept the deer's path, park the car, and turn out the lights. One man remains in the car, and the other two must be strung out along the road, one on each side of the probable crossing. When and if the deer crosses the road, the dog will probably be a quarter of a mile behind. Both men must be ready. When the dog breaks from cover onto the road, both must flash their lights on him and yell. The owner must catch him and whip him so hard that the dog realizes it doesn't pay to run deer. He must get the idea that whenever he pursues that trail, he is running right into trouble.

But this is only part of the training lesson. Every deer track offers a splendid opportunity for several lessons, and here is where the rope is used. As soon as you have disciplined your dog or just at the instant you catch him, snap the rope to his collar. Take him in one hand, your whip, flashlight, and coil of rope in the other, and walk parallel to the deer's trail, perhaps fifty feet from

it, until you have walked fifty yards more or less. Turn
and lead the dog across the trail. When you are almost
to it, let him go—but on the long leash. More than likely
he will find the track and start running it. Let him get
to the end of the rope and lean back and flop him. Haul
him in and thrash him again, scolding him and saying,
"Don't touch" as you do.

Repeat the performance, making another swing in a
half circle until you have again crossed the deer track.
If he still shows interest, discipline again. In fact, you
can go on and on with this training until he understands
that deer are not for him to run.

The selection of the training place is most important.
One of the authors has located a spot in Connecticut
where there are crossroads every half mile or less. In one
season he broke six dogs of running deer at this spot.

To the man who understands his dog, there is generally a different tone of voice for every animal pursued.
Thus, one dog barks a deep guttural growl when he
pursues and trees a porcupine. On deer, he has almost
a scream; on coon his voice is average. At the tree there
is a very great difference between the coon bark and the
porcupine bark. The former seems to have notes of ex-
hilaration, while for the latter the tone is of marked
disgust. Such inflections, if they are understood, will
prove very helpful.

These methods work, but there is a very much sim-
pler one which can be used by some. Bear in mind that
you are endeavoring to have a dog dislike the odors of
the animals you want him to let alone. He must come

to realize that trailing them is equivalent to running into severe trouble. Hence, as a sound preliminary to the above, we find that we can often proof dogs against deer, fox, stock, and rabbits by the following method.

We plant a box of rabbits on the upwind side of a hedgerow or stone wall several hundred yards long at a time when the breeze is at right angles to this wall. Seventy-five or a hundred yards farther, we plant a fox in a cage. Next is a small pen of deer bedding. Lastly is a coon track which goes at right angles to the wall and upwind to a tree.

The dog is taken on a leash downwind about forty feet from the wall. When he goes by the point where the rabbits are hidden, if he shows the slightest interest in going toward them, he is punished, as he is if he shows interest while passing the fox and deer bedding. If previous punishment has made him somewhat wary about running the coon track when he gets to it, he is urged along and the leash removed from his collar. Then, when he barks up, he is rewarded. Half a dozen such lessons help remarkably. With some dogs, it is all the training they ever need to keep them from trailing the wrong animal.

Animal scents are used successfully by some hunters to train dogs and break them too. When used for the latter purpose, the principle of satiation is employed. The dog is kept so satiated with the odor of the animal you want him to leave alone that he becomes disgusted with that animal; he just wants no more of it. Several makers of scents advertise them in hunting magazines.

If you try one, follow the directions for their use, but don't be too sure that they will be 100 per cent successful. Some hunters report remarkable cures, some report failures, and several coon hunters have told us that, in breaking dogs off fox, they have broken them off coon as well. Much conscientious effort on the part of several makers of scent has gone into their products.

We also use an electric collar which proves more effective for discipline than a whipping. An added advantage of this is that the dog blames the game for his hurt and not the trainer. Such a collar is easy to make. An induction coil is connected with two dry cells and a small rheostat and switch. These are contained in a box strapped on one's chest. The switch is on the out side of the box. Light strong cable with two wires inside runs to a dog harness from the box. The cable splits, and one wire goes to each side of a brass open collar which has two studs in each side. One set of studs is insulated, of course. Therefore, the charge goes through the dog's neck. Only a very light charge need be given; what is a very mild charge to a man may be very severe to a dog. The dog is allowed plenty of leeway and the wire is played out or hauled in so it is always kept from snarling. We have had unusual results with this outfit in some cases. It was invented by the senior author of this book as the outcome of another electrical invention which accomplished indoor training of dogs, where air was piped past various animals and thence to the dogs, by rewarding them for barking at the raccoon and shocking them through the feet and legs when they barked at the wrong animals.

Few novice trainers seem to realize the value of day-time walks with their hounds. By using a long check cord and walking a pup, you acquaint him with the woods. Often you have opportunities to show him what not to do. Squirrel hunting is one of the best introductions to coon hunting and fun for the trainer too. The natural tree dog will often have opportunities to see squirrels run and climb. He will chase them and bark, especially if given encouragement. If you throw sticks at them, that makes you part of the game; your dog realizes you are trying to help, thus establishing a partnership. In hunting season you can shoot the squirrels. His chewing them a little will not harm the meat. Soon you'll find he will become excited at squirrel tracks and bay, following them to the tree without using his eyes. Your encouragement at such times should be enthusiastic, as it will be, naturally. Many a good squirrel dog has taken to coon hunting with no other training at all.

Additional training is needed when you plan to hunt by the automobile method, which is discussed in detail in the following chapter. In the past we have trained a good many car dogs.

It is well to start the hound in country where coons almost certainly will be found. One man drives the car; the other walks in front with the dog. The driver lets the walker keep about fifty yards ahead of him. The dog soon gets used to the car lights, the hum of the motor, and the hunter's presence. After considerable walking, the trainer drops back closer and closer to the car, or the driver keeps closer to the trainer. The dog becomes accustomed to this setup.

After more walking, the trainer sits on a front mud-guard and rides, occasionally talking to the hound and cheering him along. When the dog has become used to this system, he more or less seems to regard the trainer as part of the car. It is now time for the trainer to sit inside with his head out of a window.

When another car's lights are seen either behind or ahead, the dog is called in. When the car has gone, the dog is let out again.

Soon the dog associates the speeding up of the motor with running ahead of the car and hustles out to take his position and jog along. By this time it is generally no longer necessary to ride on the mudguard. One night's training of a smart dog can have him car-trained for life. Of course, the hound must follow a few coon tracks before he knows he can have implicit confidence in you— that you won't fail him. He learns that you will stop the car and come to his calling at the tree.

Car hunting sometimes offers wonderful opportunities for training. You may see deer or fox or porcupines crossing the road, and you learn quickly just what your dog will or won't run. By speeding up the car you can often run down a dog that has jumped a deer or fox in the road, jump out, and administer punishment.

Some dogs annoy car hunters by stopping at what seems like every other bush along the road to urinate. This can be stopped by carrying a pocketful of small gravel and throwing a little of it at the dog when he stops unnecessarily. If a sharp command is given at the same time, he learns to quit at the command.

When a hunter starts out, he can expect his dog's first inclination to be to dash wildly down the road, especially if there is another dog hunting with him. This speed carries him over coon tracks he would not miss if he were going at a normal gate. For that reason, it is well to get the first half mile of a hunt over in country where coons may not be found.

From this description, you may judge that the authors have done considerable car hunting. We have, despite the fact that we condemn this method of hunting in the next chapter. However, this isn't a case of "Do as we say, not as we do," because we use this method only in localities where everyone hunts that way.

We have mentioned the simplest methods of training a coon dog. We have not touched upon the serious question of getting the dog to stay at the tree, and this is exceedingly important. It is largely a matter of confidence. Your dog will stay if he knows that you will come. You must lengthen the interval gradually. A wise coon hunter will not always go dashing to the tree immediately. He will often hold off purposely to show the dog that his calling will bring results if he waits long enough. This is much like businessmen who go to the bank and borrow money, paying it back when they say they will and thus establishing confidence in the minds of the bankers. They do not always need the money, but that unblemished record on the bank books and in the banker's mind stands them in good stead when the time of need arises.

Don't rush up to the dog. Let him bark an hour sometimes, when you have time. Then when you need to have him bark half the night, he is more likely to do so. When you have found him after such an episode, you and he are partners for certain.

Probably most coon dogs are trained by running in packs with tried and true older cooners, or at least with one older dog. The dog being trained is kept on a leash until the trained dog bays. The pup is liberated and runs to the sound of the older dog's voice, joining him in following the trail. This teaches him only that coon trails are fun to follow—not that he must run only coon trails. The negative aspects must usually be carried out too, for a spirited pup so loves to follow any animal's spoor that he must be broken from following those which you want him to ignore.

The delight which the dog feels at having pleased the man whom he respects as his master, coupled with knowing what pleases his master and what does not, makes the coon dog, provided he has the heredity that enables him to do what you want him to do. Make a strong bond of friendship between you. Don't be high-hat to him, but be the master at all times. Gain his respect and confidence, and you have done a great deal to win his loyalty and affection.

Porcupine problems. In at least a quarter of the states of the United States, porcupines are an ever-present threat to new coon dogs. Several lessons are required before a dog learns not to attack one, and several more are needed to teach a dog not to follow a porcupine trail or even bark at a porcupine when he winds it, comes upon it in his ranging, or perhaps sees it climbing a tree—a temptation almost too strong for any dog to resist. But for all the temptation, the dog learns with proper coaching.

No one in his right mind would take a new cooner into porcupine country without first having coached the dog and shown him how absurd it is to "tie into" one. Any hunter can get a porcupine. They can be found near ledges and are easy to trap in their caves. They can be treed by dogs which know enough not to attack them.

A small chain with a ring in one end can be used to circle the porky's middle and then pulled tight. Wearing high leather tops or puttees, step on the porcupine's tail close to the body. The tail is his active weapon; the body quills are his protection. A slight touch on the back and that powerful tail flips upward sideways and drives the small black quills, with which it is filled, into the body of your dog or into your leg. If you have a foot on the tail, the porcupine has no weapon.

While you do this, a companion lets your dog, who must know what "Don't touch" means, ease up toward the porcupine. He will get some quills in his nose if you both play your parts properly. These are pulled. After a few lessons the dog realizes that the quills pain him while going in and that having them pulled is an inexorable consequence. He decides the porcupine is interesting but not to be trusted.

You then take him by the sides of the head and push his nose onto some quills as if you are punishing him for his actions, and that adds a final touch—especially pulling the quills.

The next lesson is to let the dog watch this new interest waddle off and climb a tree. When the porcupine is safely out of the dog's reach, ancher it with the chain and let the dog go. If he runs to the tree and barks up, scold him, whip him a little, and take him away. Let him go again. He'll probably tree again. Go to him and chain him. Climb up and pull the "quill pig" down and let the hound find out how it really feels to attack a porcupine. Quite often this will be all the lesson he'll ever need. You are there yelling "Don't touch!" and he is finding out that disobeying you is fraught with disastrous consequences.

When you hunt with your dog and he trees a porcupine, chain him the first time, shake out the animal, and see what he does with it. If he doesn't attack it, get a foot on it or kill it and stick the dog's nose into it so that he comes to know he is going to get hurt for misbehaving. He'll then leave porcupines alone entirely. Each time he trees one, scold him; you may break a smart dog completely in one day and night.

We took five tough cooners into Maine, spent one afternoon educating each, and had five dogs that wouldn't even tree a porcupine before two nights had passed. Once or twice, at first, they "treed" one on the ground—that was all. We have broken many dogs by this method. It works.

For the benefit of those who have never pulled quills, some pointers may not be amiss. The quill, under a microscope, looks along its barbed point like a thistle with scales, each overlapping the next. The point is sharper than most needles, being a hard, tough, modified hair. When the point is driven into the dog's flesh by the porcupine's tail or from the dog's attacking the animal, the barbs prevent it from dropping out. The muscle fibers of the dog twitch and keep moving the quill along, usually turning it so that it runs lengthwise. For example, quills in the front leg muscles tend to go up or down. If up, they work until they reach the shoulder blades and end up sticking out of the skin at the withers (the high point of the shoulders).

Quills which get into a joint, especially the wrist joint, may stay many months. Sometimes one will keep working in muscles for months. Those about the head may penetrate an eye. Those in the chest may work into the heart. We have found young coons dead from porcupine quills in some vital organ and many others with quills which had not killed them.

Assuming you would not venture into the woods without quill pullers (the most effective type is described in Chapter 10), what do you do if your dog is severely quilled?

1. Chain him so he can't run away.

2. Don't let him lie down and roll the quills in.

3. Pull the body quills first—all you can get. If you break one off, don't let it stop you from pulling all you can.

4. Sit down against a tree. Throw the dog across one leg and wrap the other about his middle. Squeeze. Hold him so he can't get loose, and you and your assistants pull head quills and any that are in the wrist joints. Pull the quills out of the mouth. Those in the lips can be pushed through and pulled out point first. Those between the teeth and in the gums come out easily. Those in the tongue can be pulled by grasping the tongue, after covering the hand with soil from the ground to prevent slipping, and pulling the tongue out so you can get hold of the quills. You may have such a savage dog that he will need a one-inch-thick stick held between his jaws until his mouth is empty of quills, after which you can tie his mouth closed and proceed to pull quills from wherever they are. Lots of them, in a bad quilling, will have worked in out of sight before you've had a chance to pull them.

Some hunters clip the quills off at the skin, others douse them with mineral oil, and still others say that kerosene kills them. We have not found these remedies effective, however. Some say the quills come easily if you twist them out, but even this we find helps but little with a deep-set quill.

The big white ones can often be pulled in clusters since so small a proportion is barb; the little black tail quills are what give most of the trouble.

A badly quilled dog is in a state of shock. Keep him warm after you've pulled all the quills you can. Next day feel him all over and pull the quills that have worked out.

If the details of training a coon dog not too touch porcupines seem cruel to anyone, we freely agree. But when an untrained dog has to be subjected to the ordeal of quilling and the necessary pulling, the training, anyone would say, is a pink tea by comparison.

In Chapter 11 on taking raccoons alive, we have advocated the use of Nembutal, which you have to get from your veterinarian or physician. It would be an excellent thing if every coon hunter carried it when his dogs are not porcupine-broken. If an injection is given at the dosage of 1 cc to each five pounds of the dog's weight into a vein of the front leg, he will go at once into a deep sleep. All the muscles will cease movement, and the quills will not move. They can be pulled out with no pain to the dog and with a much higher percentage of quills recovered. But the dog must be carried home or to the car since he won't come to for many hours.

If a hunter does not know how to strike a vein, he can inject the Nembutal into the abdomen, and the effect will take place in ten to fifteen minutes instead of in a matter of seconds.

9. *How to Hunt Coons*

COON HUNTING is a matter of sharp wits and a good dog.
After what we have said about training a dog, it is
hardly necessary to give detailed instructions about the
hunt; but there are certain matters of interest which
will not always occur to a beginner and which experienced coon hunters sometimes overlook. First, we shall
consider the two general methods of hunting, and then
we can take up the details. Some hunters train their

dogs to range out in search of game while they sit and talk, and others train their dogs to hunt while they walk. There are arguments on both sides. Sometimes the two methods can be combined judiciously. There is also a third method which in our estimation should be outlawed in all states—what we call the automobile method.

The ranging method. Where a hunting territory is broad and where coons range over a wide section, such as a river bottom or broad valley, it is very handy to be able to sit down and know your dog is out hunting game. This, besides being the finest way to hunt, gives an excellent opportunity for telling stories, getting acquainted, and making friendships. Before an owner can hunt this way, however, his dog must be well trained and a natural ranger.

A hunting party using the ranging method will go into a territory and choose a spot to sit down, letting the dog strike out by himself. Usually the dog does not go far ahead but travels more often in a sideways direction. He may cover half a mile or more across. He uses his nose and can catch the air drift from a coon hundreds of yards away. If, after hunting over such a territory, the dog finds no coons, he will return to the party and generally shake his head. The owner will proudly inform any neophytes present that the dog has found nothing and has come to say so by shaking his head.

Then the party gets up and starts for another spot half a mile or so away, sits down, and lets the dog range. Hunters have to be alert for distant barking, because a wide-ranging dog may be gone for an hour or more in country he knows well. Intoxicating liquors are out so far as a coon hunter is concerned. They numb the senses, and no man half under from whiskey will get the enjoyment he should from the hunt. If he comes to drink and not to hunt, he should be allowed to congregate with his own kind and not with hunters who go for the sport of the hunt, who want to hear and see great dogs do their work in a masterful way. A coon hunt is definitely not the place for drink.

If the dog barks, the hunters must get to the tree, no matter how far or how hard the going. It is the feeling on the part of the dog that his master will never desert him, never fool him, that makes him willing to stay at the tree. Once that feeling of security is broken, the hunter can no longer be assured that the dog will stay. If he leaves the tree, the coon will be down and away in a very short time. On one occasion, one of us lost his dog when the wind came up and the dog had ranged very far away. The party hunted for four hours and finally heard him more than a mile away barking tree. We rushed as fast as we could to the spot, and, when we got near the tree, the dog came bounding up to see us because he was so happy that we had come. Almost immediately he dashed back to show us the tree, but in that instant the coon had gotten out of the tree and run straight to a den tree not far away. We lost him.

On the whole, the ranging method is the best way to hunt. In some sections hunters even build fires. On another occasion, one of us went to a southern state and hunted at the Negro penitentiary farm. We had two lifers with us as trusties, and they carried our ax and saw and a gallon of fuel oil. Every time we stopped for the dogs to range, the trusties went to work cutting down a few small trees and made a fire by throwing some fuel oil on them. We kept warm, but this was not too good in the long run. We found ourselves very cold as soon as we left the fire. The theory was that we would walk so fast getting to the tree when the dogs barked that we would stay warm. Unfortunately the dogs didn't bark, and most of the night was spent building fires.

Frequently hunters who have wide-ranging dogs will forget their obligation to such dogs and will continue to walk instead of sitting down and waiting. When they do, they shake the dog's confidence. We are dealing with a fine mechanism when we handle a great coon dog, and we cannot be too careful about the consequences of our actions. It is a simple matter to ruin a wide ranger by walking, so that when he comes in from a hunt he does not find us waiting. Instead, he has to hunt for us after having hunted for coons, and the two do not mix well. It is imperative, therefore, that we forsake our own comfort and sit there to wait, even if we are cold.

The more we consider the many things to be kept in mind, the less we have to wonder that some people, because of their intelligence and their "way with dogs," nearly always have good coon dogs, while others, because of a lack of these qualities, never have good dogs unless someone else has trained them. Even then, it is often not very long before they have ruined the dog.

The walking method. A great many dogs are trained so that the owner has to walk continually to get them to hunt at all. Probably more than half of all coon dogs are this kind. They can be trained sometimes to range out, but generally such training requires that the dog be young, and usually a year or more passes before the dogs will really range properly.

Hunters who walk with their dogs must depend upon *their own* intelligence in taking their dogs where coons are most plentiful and then remaining in territory where they are most likely to congregate. For instance, it is always wise to plot a hunt which will take the hunters along a road which goes between the living places and the feeding places of the quarry. For instance, here, we know, is a long mountain full of ledges, along the bottom of which is a wood or a dirt road very seldom traveled. On the other side of the road is a brook and, beyond the brook, a swamp in which we have seen tracks during the summer. It is reasonably certain that the coons have come from the hill or mountain and gone out to feed in the swamp. So we would think the road a most excellent place to hunt if we are going to walk, because our dog would be reasonably sure to cross the track of a coon as it went from its den to its feeding grounds. Or, for example, suppose that we know a level plain with large den trees. Nearby is a mountain on which are many oaks and nut trees. If we want to walk in such a way as to insure our greatest chance of finding game, we should walk in a line between the mountain and the den trees. We might select a brook where we be-

lieve there are coons and walk along its bank. Later on
we shall consider in detail the places to hunt, but this
must always be considered in hunting by whatever
method we use. It is especially true when we walk continually.

The automobile method. We mention this method
only to condemn it. It is not new. Years ago the lazy
hunters and the meat hogs used horses and wagons. The
method consists of training a dog to hunt ahead of an
automobile and driving the automobile at from five to
twenty miles an hour while the dog stays in the light of
the headlights where he can be seen by the men in the
car. Some dogs will run as fast as twenty miles an hour,
keeping it up hour after hour; but most dogs can do no
better than ten or twelve.

When you see the hound stop suddenly, you stop the
car and watch. His actions tell you whether he has a
track. He may run out a few dozen yards or more in the
wrong direction and then turn to follow it properly. If
he is an open trailer, you will hear as well as see that he
has a coon's trail.

Such trails are generally fresher than those found in
the woods; the trail must be fairly fresh for a dog to
acknowledge it when he is trotting at ten miles an hour
across it—not in the direction of it.

For those who want to use this system of hunting, we
have discussed the training of the car dog in Chapter
8.

It will be, we hope, "the thing" to take all raccoon

alive. The method is not difficult and has the following advantages:

1. You know what you have before you kill it. With the new plans under way for the liberation of dark raccoon in several states and with the natural interest in coon hunting and bettering the stock on the part of every real sportsman, it is foolish to blaze away at every coon just because you see a pair of eyes. Literally thousands of dollars' worth of beautiful black coons, albinos, and chestnuts have been ruthlessly killed because hunters whose dogs treed them did not realize at what they were shooting.

2. You will be able to restock your own hunting grounds. It pays to bring all the females home alive and kill the inferior males. We should like to see it made illegal to kill female coons; if this were done, a new impetus would be given to coon hunting. All coons would then have to be taken alive. This cannot come about in the present state of education and experience of the average coon hunter, but if you are wise you will bring home all the females and keep them in a pen until the season is over, liberating them in your own hunting ground to restock it. This is what both the authors do.

3. You do not destroy baby coons. When a hunter standing on the ground looks into a tree, sees a pair of eyes reflecting in the glare of his flashlight, and shoots at those eyes, he often brings to ground a tiny kitten. The raccoon has two mating seasons. If she misses the February season, she mates again in the spring, bringing forth kittens in August. Baby coons born in August are

still only kittens when October or November arrives. We have seen them at this season so small that they could hardly get about in a tree. One of them actually fell out of a tree when the mother had rushed them all up, and the dog caught it in his mouth before it struck the ground. This baby weighed three pounds. Hundreds of these little animals are killed every year in the United States because hunters do not take the trouble to see the game before they shoot. Their pelts are not worth removing, and every one killed means that there will be one less mature coon to hunt the next fall.

4. You may obtain a prize. Many a hunter has wished a thousand times that he had not shot a certain coon. One pelt, exhibited at a coon supper in Connecticut, was black with a sprinkling of white hairs, as beautiful as any silver fox, and large too. The hunter sold it for $15. Had he kept it alive, bred from it, and perpetuated this coloration, he might have turned that idle shot into a thousand dollars. Many a man has shot red, white, and other colored raccoons and wished too late that he had not.

To take a raccoon alive is not at all difficult. There are many ways of doing it. Some are brutal and some very kindly; these are the ways we have tried:

The net method. By using a fish seine with meshes about two inches apart, it is rather easy to capture a coon, provided the tree into which it has gone is not over a bad lot of undergrowth. If it is, the undergrowth must be cleared away to permit free handling of the net. Two or three hunters hold the net, spreading it out as widely as possible. One hunter must hold the light and keep it up on the coon, not down in the eyes of the men holding the net. An inexperienced man will think first of all about watching the coon himself. Actually he is the least important member, and his job is to keep the light out of the eyes of the net holders and yet permit them to see the coon as long as possible. Then man who climbs the tree must shake the coon out, and the men on the ground must attempt to catch it in the net. As soon as it strikes the net, the holders bring their hands together, and the coon is in a porous sack. He will chew out in no time unless this is then dropped into a strong sack out of which he cannot chew. Sometimes the coon will slide down the outside branches of a tree and drop past the net. Occasionally he will drop on one of the holders or land so that it is impossible for him to be caught in the center. Then it is often necessary to snap the net over him quickly and tangle him up in its meshes. One holder must know in advance that it is his job to do this.

The dog method. If you have a dog that will hold a coon, teach him what "Don't touch" means; and have him know it so well that he will drop the coon at your command. It is not difficult to do and a good responsible dog will soon get to learn that this is his job. One of us has a dog which knows just when to let go; and, as soon as the coon is safely in the sack, off he goes, hunting again. He has learned that his part is over then and there, and he participates in the whole affair like a veteran.

If more than one dog is used in the hunt, all but one should be tied to trees. Then the climber should go up and shake out the coon; and the trained dog will parry until he can catch him by the side of the throat. The hunter then catches the coon by the tail and puts one foot on the coon's shoulder where the dog is holding on. Thus he holds the coon pinned to the ground and, at the same time, pushes the dog's head off the neck, saying "Don't touch" to the dog. The dog lets go; and, if the coon is not too large, it can be held there indefinitely. The sack holders have the sack ready, and the coon is quickly lifted and plunged downward into it. This method requires three or four men to carry it out. One man has to climb, one handles the coon, and two hold the sack, which, it goes without saying, should be one with a wide mouth. Ordinary burlap is good enough if the coon does not have to stay in it too long.

In case there are only three men, one man has to hold the bag in two places, and the man who handles the coon has to reach out with one hand and catch the mouth of the bag to make a triangle of it and plunge the coon in. The word "plunge" is the right one to describe it; the animal cannot be placed in gently because his sharp claws will reach and catch the bag almost every time.

In handling the coon, it is often necessary to shake him hard so that he will not reach up with his front paws and climb up on his fur until he reaches the hand of the holder and bite it severely. A coon can bite right through a man's hand. He can crack finger bones with his teeth and should be handled with every precaution.

There are times when only two men will be hunting together and when it is desirable to catch the coon alive. Both the authors can handle the largest coon either has ever seen alive without any help whatever, and place the animal in a sack single-handed. The way we do it is this:

As soon as we make the dog let go, we take the coon by the tail, swing him over the shoulder, and smack him against the ground on his belly. This will not hurt him but will stun him momentarily. Instantly we kneel on him, putting one knee on each side of his shoulders and crossing our toes in back of his hind end so he cannot back out. Then we can cautiously reach the first and second fingers of our hand under his jaw and clamp the hand about the face so he cannot bite. The second finger is pressed in the V under the jaw so it makes a secure hold. Then we tie a cord around the face and head, take a sack by the bottom and push the bottom up through the mouth. We take hold of the coon's tail near its base, clutching it through the bag, and lift the coon up suddenly. Then it is possible to pull the bag down around him and gather the mouth together, and the coon is captured. One of us captured a twenty-seven-pound coon by this method.

The forked-stick method. In nearly every party of coon hunters there will be found someone who starts whittling a crotched stick as soon as a dog trees a coon. The idea is to slip the stick over the coon's neck while the dog is facing it or when the dog has caught it. Just where this old notion came from, goodness only knows —it is far easier and kinder to catch a coon by the tail and slam its head on a stone or against a tree trunk than to hold him with a crotched stick and allow a dog to munch on the coon until he is dead.

A forked or crotched stick is all well and good, provided it works. All hunters have probably seen a man try to put such a stick on a coon. Often the coon backs up and the man lands on his head. The neck of the coon is very large, and usually a forked stick will slip off over his head. Trying to use one to catch a coon alive is senseless, as far as our experience is concerned, despite the fact that so much is heard about it.

The hollow-tree method. In many states it is against the law to touch a coon in a den tree. This is as it should be. The law represents the rules of the game. Generally the law is about twenty years behind schedule, but it does serve as a guide. The hollow tree should be considered as the end of the hunt. No coon should be disturbed in one, nor should any be cut down. To walk through the woods and see where great trees have been sawed down to get out a paltry five dollars' worth of coon pelt and a little meat makes one stop and think what a crime that is, but it is even worse to think that this tree was the coon's home and now the home has been destroyed. Chopping down trees for wild bees is just as bad, as these trees too are generally useful as coon dens. It is not at all uncommon to find bees and coons in the same tree. Coon hunters should campaign for laws which will prevent hunters of any kind from chopping down the old forest monarchs. However, there are states where the practice is allowed, and there are coon hunters who are not sportsmen enough to leave the trees.

At times, when woods are being cut for lumber, coons are found nestled in a den. They may be driven out by putting a rag soaked in melted sulfur into the cavity, or the tree may be sawed in two parallel cuts and a section split out large enough to allow someone to reach in. A one-inch iron pipe, through which a stout wire has been looped, will serve as an excellent tool to remove the coons. The wire should run through the pipe and be looped out of one end. This loop can be pushed over a coon's head and the ends pulled tight through the pipe and held. Then the coon may be removed—with plenty of effort.

The anesthetic method. There is one way of capturing coons alive which is so simple and humane that we think every coon hunter who wants to bring 'em back alive should be able and equipped to use it. We refer to the use of anesthetics.

If a proper-size dose of one of the injectible so-called barbiturates is injected into the animal, he goes to sleep and can be painlessly captured with very little danger to the hunter or damage to the coon.

Of all the drugs we have tried, sodium pentabarbital seems to offer the most advantages. It goes by the trade name of Nembutal. Veterinarians make up solutions themselves or buy it already mixed in 100-cc bottles.

Any veterinarian will let you have a bottle and help you out with a syringe if you tell him how you propose to use it. You need a 5-cc syringe and a 1½-inch long 20-gauge needle to use in injecting the drug.

The syringe is marked with five graduations to each cc. Since the dose to produce complete anesthesia is 1 cc to each five pounds of weight, each graduation equals one pound. All you need to do is estimate the coon's weight as closely as possible, fill the springe to the proper mark, and plunge the needle into the coon's abdomen, not into the muscles or skin or fat but into the abdomen proper. Then you press the plunger which forces the Nembutal out and all around the intestines. It is quickly absorbed, and in five or ten minutes your coon is so dead to the world that you can pick him up and carry him home draped over your arm, in a bag, or in your hunting coat—all with no danger of being bitten. He will not be completely conscious for six hours, if you have injected the proper dose. If you give too much he won't ever wake up.

Now to discuss how to handle the coon up to the time you inject him. We assume you have treed him or dug him out and at least can catch hold of his tail. If you can get hold of a coon's tail in a tree, he'll hang to the tree generally so hard that he won't feel the prick of the needle. You can inject him and wait until he is about to fall. Hold him over a limb until he is dead to the world. We have done this several times, usually in evergreens where the coon has gone right to the top.

Usually the coon will be out on a lateral limb where

he can't be reached. Then he must be shaken out or the limb cut off, if it is a small one, and the coon caught on the ground. Once the coon is on the ground, he must be held by the tail with a foot on his neck. The dog must be trained to let go when told to, or an assistant must be ready to choke him off if he won't let go.

It is easy to turn the coon so his belly is exposed and to plunge the syringe needle through the skin and muscles. The wait for loss of consciousness is not long.

Any hunter using this humane method will not want to use any other, especially in capturing larger coons. We think that such equipment is more than worth while anyway, because in emergencies with a dog, such as porcupine quillings, rents in abdomens by bobcats, and so forth, Nembutal can be used to excellent advantage.

When a coon has been brought home, it is not an easy matter to get a collar on him. Neither is it an easy matter to catch hold of the ring in the collar when one desires to take the coon from the cage. We have found that a coon which is to be used for laying trails or removed for exercise had better have two chain links on the collar, the second link hanging from the first. The long hair generally prevents the first from being seen, but the second will hang down enough to be visible, while not hampering the coon in any way.

We have used several ways to put the collar on the animal. One way is: drive him into a box, loop a wire under the body, pull the coon up against the wire at the top, place another wire under the neck tight against the top wire, and place the collar on, being careful to keep away from the coon's teeth. The hand must be reached inside the box and the collar must be put on fairly tight, or the coon will slip it over his head.

There is another way which appears to be difficult but is really simple. Go into the pen with a burlap bag folded twice lengthwise, making really eight thicknesses of bag. Hold one end in each hand and scare the coon so that he walks upside down on the wire on top the cage. Reach up and grab him just behind the front shoulders with the bag. This acts as a pad and also prevents him from turning his head enough to reach your hand. Quickly flop him on the bottom of the cage and kneel on the folded bag. This holds him securely against the ground, and your toes crossed behind him prevent him from wiggling out backward. Then the fingers are worked carefully around so the second finger is under the jaw and the thumb clamps down on top. The coon is secure, and if he is held firmly against the ground, he cannot draw his claws backward enough to scratch even if he does hook them over your hand.

If one attempts to collar a coon in this way, there had better not be more than one coon in the pen, since a mate will frequently attack a man who seems to be maltreating another coon. This has often happened to the authors when they have been handling coons.

It is the practice with some coon owners to cut off the fangs, so that if one is bitten by a coon there are no bad gashes or deep wounds. This is a simple matter. The coon must be held and a sharp chisel placed against the inside of the tooth. Another is placed against the outside opposite to it, and the outside one struck a sharp blow with a hammer. The tooth will pop off. This is repeated for all four fangs. The results are good so far as the owner is concerned, but the exposed nerves are extremely painful to the raccoon. Generally these stubs decay and finally drop out, although this is not always the case. It is much better to anesthetize the animal and extract the fangs. When he comes to, he will feel pain for several days, but that will be all.

10. *Coon Hunting Equipment*

A MAN WHO receives an invitation to go coon hunting for the first time usually replies that it has been a long time since he did any shooting and that he hasn't the proper equipment anyway. That is the answer to be expected from those ignorant of coon hunting. Actually, the necessary equipment, besides the dog, which is taken for granted, is not much trouble to assemble.

One must have a pair of warm waterproof shoes which come up as close to the knees as possible. After trying every kind that we could find, we have come to the conclusion that the best types are: (1) Those with a leather top and rubber bottom joined by several rows of stitching and plenty of cement between. There are many makes on the market. Some companies make very light ones and some make them with or without heels. Our experience dictates shoes with heels of the strongest rubber obtainable. Such a pair of shoes has already lasted one of us for two entire seasons, and the tops have lasted five years. (2) Shoes made completely—feet and tops—of rubber. True, they tear easier than leather, but can be vulcanized.

For tree climbing the long uppers act as guards, leather tops somewhat more than the rubber tops. For wading brooks, the sixteen-inch top on either is by far the best and most comfortable in the long run. For warmth, it is better to buy shoes a half-size larger than usual so that there is room for two pairs of heavy woolen socks on the very cold nights. Good shoes are essential, as there is nothing quite so disconcerting to a party of coon hunters as having one of the members grumbling about cold feet. It makes the hunt unpleasant for everyone concerned.

The next most important item of equipment is a pair of pants of material so stout and strong that it will withstand tears from briars, twigs, prickers, and rough tree bark. Such trousers are usually of very heavy cotton duck with a double thickness over the knees and thighs. We have found that this material is quite clammy when wet, and we wear a pair of light woolen trousers under the pants in cold weather.

It is best by all odds to leave heavy sweaters at home and wear clothing that can be opened in the front. On cold nights when one has to exercise briskly, running up a mountainside or hill, one will perspire freely and soak any undergarments which are worn. At such times it is best to be wearing a coat, jacket, or lumberjack which can be opened to allow cool traveling. Then, when the peak of the hill is gained and there is time for resting and cooling off, these heavy outer jackets can be buttoned gradually with no discomfort from damp undergarments. We do not believe that sitting well drenched in perspiration gives one pneumonia or even a cold, because we have never known that to happen. We are thinking solely about the comfort of the hunter.

Regarding garments that open in front, a heavy lumberjack should be worn over the shirt. A sheepskin coat is the best thing we have found to top this off. It should have a sheepskin-lined collar. Leather coats are fine, provided they do not have leather collars. Such a collar becomes too clammy to be tolerated. The coat should not be of the short type; the forty-four-inch length is the best we have found. This equipment is necessary only for those hunting in cold climates; in the South there would be no need for it.

Guns can be considered next. The kind of gun carried depends upon many considerations. If the hunters are a lazy lot, a shotgun and No. 2 shells are satisfactory in the early fall when the leaves are on and it is difficult to sight the coon. In the later fall, lazy hunters can take a .22 caliber rifle, and a good marksman can hit a coon between the eyes eight times out of ten. But the best way, we think, is to carry a small revolver in your pocket and climb the tree. A .32 is large enough, though not too large. After getting as close to the coon as possible, it will be a simple matter to hit it in the head. It falls out of the tree unconscious.

We prefer, whenever possible, to bring the coons home alive; and to do this we carry two large-mouthed burlap bags of heavy material, a small lot of string, and a good sharp knife. Besides this, we have a very large fish hook with which we can drag a dead coon out from under a ledge if we have to shoot it. This is on a small chain, but can be attached to a stick; we have often used it in this way. In addition, we carry a 100-foot piece of quarter-inch Irish linen rope. This has been tested for 600 pounds capacity, and the entire roll of it can be put around the waist without one's realizing that he is carrying anything.

When we hunt in the North, we carry porcupine pliers to pull quills from any dogs that may have been attacked by those pesky creatures. We use pointed electrician's pliers or surgical hemostats with jaws which meet closely, as it is necessary to catch hold of bloody quills and the tweezers must not slip off.

It is an excellent idea for a hunter to be equipped with a supply of Nembutal with a syringe and needle, as explained in the preceding chapter, both for use in capturing live coons and for pulling porcupine quills from hunting dogs in a painless manner. In an anesthetized dog, the quills stop moving inward, because there is no muscle movement and quills do not, in themselves, possess any ability to move.

Lights are another important consideration. The three- and five-cell flashlights are excellent, the five-cell seeming to be the most economical in the long run. From tests, we have discovered that the five-cell flashlight will furnish sufficient light to enable us to get through the woods for three entire nights or four fairly long nights. The three-cell light does not last quite three-fifths as long. The two-cell light is not objectionable, but is not as economical as the others. A good point about the others is that one can carry a supply of fresh batteries in the pocket and use them only when brightest illumination is needed, removing them when through and inserting the partially used batteries. When the old ones are entirely used up, the new ones will have been somewhat used and they can be exhausted in turn. New bulbs should also be part of the equipment of every hunter. We each carry an extra bulb in the caps of our flashlights.

A recent valuable addition to the available lights is a flat eight-cell affair which fits in a coat pocket. It is adjustable and uses any number of dry cells depending on the volume of light required. Used for flashing trees a single filling with dry cells will last a whole season for the average hunter. The light is widely advertised and more than lives up to claims made for it.

Small acetylene torches which attach to one's cap are dangerous because they are exposed and can set fires. Everyone in the hunting party is annoyed by it when the wearer turns to speak.

An electric lantern can be had with a bulb and globe within a protector that covers the bottom as well as the front. It may be focused to a spot and throws the beam a very long distance. It holds four flashlight batteries.

The old-fashioned barn lantern had better be left at home unless your state law requires that you carry one. If it can be secured with a shield which is absolutely impervious to light, then it is not so bad, provided the carrier will remember to keep the shield behind the light and not turn it sideways. The bright light from a lantern is extremely disagreeable to all who walk behind it, and it takes a great deal of consideration on the part of the bearer to prevent much annoyance to his companions.

A box of matches in a waterproof case is a handy addition to equipment. In case one of the party falls into a pond or has to go in to rescue a dog from a coon that has climbed on the dog's head, a good fire is welcome. Getting partially dry after such an experience is much better than shivering all the way home or continuing to hunt in wet clothes.

No coon hunter should venture forth without a compass. This little instrument will save hundreds of miles of walking in a season. Despite the fact that in nearly every party someone will be found who declares that compasses are always wrong, they will lead you out by the shortest way in every case, if you have learned the locations of the roads before you enter the woods. There are all kinds of compasses. The best can be very expensive and no more reliable for a coon hunter than a ten-cent variety. Better get one with an indicator.

11. *Disposal of the Coon*

ONCE THE COON has been brought home, the question of disposal arises—what is the best method of removing the skin and preparing it for market or for tanning? Coon hides are sold raw in the open market. The market for tanned hides is another proposition entirely, and every coon hunter should realize this fact. Raw skins can be sold in small lots, but tanned skins are sold in lots based on sorting and matching. The coon hunter cannot very well break into this market and should remember that, so long as conditions and customs in the fur business are as we find them today, he is a coon hunter and not a fur merchant.

Many times a hunter will realize that the fur market is low, and he may feel reasonably sure that the following year will bring an increase in prices. So he waits for a rise which doesn't come during the winter. Before he knows it, spring is upon him, market demands are limited, and he cannot unload his skins. He realizes that hot weather will ruin the skins and that he must do something. He sends the skins to the tannery, which may charge him anywhere from 25 cents to $1.25 each, depending on the kind of job he expects and the kind of tannery he has chosen. In due time his skins come back. The great big fine ones that he prizes so highly will possibly have a few spots where the hair has slipped. Another few may have holes in them where moths have nibbled, unbeknownst to him. Another few will look so much smaller than they did originally that he is convinced the tannery has substituted some other skins for his lovely ones.

One of the principal complaints received by tanneries is that they have returned the wrong skins. This they practically never do; but just for the sake of everyone's peace of mind, it is best for hunters who send hides to a tanner to mark them in some way. A few punches in one of the leg sections will serve very nicely.

Another complaint is that the tanning process has caused the hair to loosen and fall out. The tanning process is only indirectly responsible for this; the real reason is that the skin was not properly scraped and dried, and, when this is so, the hair will nearly always slip.

After all is said and done, it will be found best to make every effort to sell the hides in the raw fur market; this is the logical way. If, on the other hand, you cannot, then have them tanned. If a friend wants a neckpiece made, of course, they must be tanned. If you do find them on your hands, all nicely tanned, there is one recourse open to you—sell them to local furriers. The raw fur merchant does not want tanned hides. He is not used to handling them, and, just because you may have paid a dollar to have them tanned, they are not worth a plugged nickel more to him than they would have been in the raw. Moreover, he has learned all the little ways to beat the hunter. He has learned leverages with which he can pry the price down, leverages which are missing in the tanned hide. He will look a skin over and see a little place where it is not white but blue. He will look at another which is pretty muddy and call it a scrub, whereas if the skin were tanned, he would never see the mud and would not have that leverage. He will see a great many things that would never occur to the ordinary person, and few of these things are left in the tanned skin.

Take the question of the blue hide, for example. A little blueness does not hurt the skin, but it does hurt the price. To the buyer it indicates that the hide was taken too early, an idea which is all nonsense. Every hunter can remember blue hides taken in January which were in magnificent coat. He need not expect the buyer to believe him when he exhibits the hide and tells him it was taken in January. In theory, blue hides are those taken before the first of November, but many are the lovely white hides taken in October. Even the locality seems to have little to do with this—coons taken well up in the North late in the season have really been blue, while others taken in the South early have been fine and white. However, it is the skin buyer's stock-in-trade argument that the blue hide is worth much less. The tanning process cheats him out of that, and naturally this interferes with some of his profit. All in all, try to sell your skins early and yet not too early, or the buyer will say they were taken before they were at their best and will not pay a fair price. Certainly it is wise to sell them as soon after the close of the hunting season as possible.

We have mentioned the buyer first because he is the man to be pleased. It is on account of the buyer that skins are stretched in certain ways. It is on his account that they are split open or shipped cased. For that reason, get in touch with the fairest man in your locality and ask him what he wants and how he wants it. He will probably be echoing the demands of the house for whom he buys. You will then be safe and will please the majority of buyers.

We are strongly of the opinion that most coon hunters' associations have missed one of their most excellent opportunities in not pooling their skins and marketing them cooperatively. A splendid little business could be done in this way. If all the skins were marked and pooled, the buyers, at the end of the season, could be notified to come and bid on the lot, giving quotations on each skin. Each association would then become a small fur-auction business. In this way, better buyers could be reached. Every fur house has two lists. One of these is the price which their agents can pay, and the other list is the amount that they will pay the agents. The association would become the agent, and it would thus pay the buyers from the fur centers to go some distance to bid. It is a certainty that higher bids would result from such a system of marketing. Preseason talks by buyers on preparing and storing skins make interesting features for a meeting, too.

There are two chief ways of skinning a coon, and both are satisfactory. Some hunters use one way efficiently and some the other. To perform either operation, a good skinning knife is required. We can learn more from taxidermists about this work than from any other persons. They generally use two knives. We shall not describe the technical processes but rather the simplest, most efficient, and most practical ways of skinning.

One knife should be long-bladed with a curve in the cutting edge. The other knife should have a long blade with a slightly curved edge to be used as a scraping knife in removing surplus fat (called fleshing).

The first way we shall describe involves using a table. Place the coon on its back and make an incision in the skin the entire length of the belly from the middle of the lower lip to the anus. Circle the anus with the cut and continue down the tail about three-quarters of the way. Then, starting on one side of the belly, begin skinning, keeping as close to the skin as possible and leaving all the fat you can on the animal. When you have detached about two inches of skin, tack this to the table with three strong tacks and skin some more. In this way, you can hold the body in one hand to stretch and skin with the other hand. When you have removed enough so that the legs are being stretched, insert the point of the knife under the skin at the junction of the foreleg, and push it close to the skin and outward toward the hand, keeping as near the bottom of the leg as possible. Skin out the leg right down to the hand and cut it off at the hand, leaving the hand on the skin. Some fur buyers will tell you this is superfluous, but some ask for the skinning to be done in this way. Suit your market and not yourself in this particular.

Having done this, start on the hind leg, beginning at the anus, and again making the cut up to the foot, and skin out the leg. It is then time to tackle the tail. This should be done by very carefully cutting around the bone and freeing the skin until it is done right to the tip or as much of the way as you want. Most men have enough strength in their fingers to be able to pull the bones out of the skin when they have skinned a young coon's tail out halfway or less. Unless you have strong fingers and can pinch the skin tightly against the bone while pulling with the other hand, better not attempt this method of removing the bones.

Next, skin the head out, cutting the ears off at the skull and very carefully skinning around the eyes so that the black rim of flesh which composes the eyelids is left. Be sure not to cut the nose off. Roll the coon gradually and skin as you go until the hide is all off. This is one popular method of skinning, and a good experienced hand can finish a large-size coon in twenty minutes in this way.

The other way consists of hanging the coon up by the back feet or by one back foot at a time and skinning him in that position. A permanent string with a noose in the end is generally left hanging from a place in the ceiling or rafters where the skinning is done. One of the coon's hind feet is placed in this noose so it catches the leg just above the heel. Then the knife is inserted under the skin of the opposite leg at the heel, and it is pushed forward toward the anus. It is then run around the anus and the leg is skinned out. The tail is completed as described above. The leg is removed from the noose and the other leg placed in it so that the first leg may be skinned out. When these three operations have been completed, the skin will fall downward, and the hunter places one hand inside where he can catch hold of the dry fur and pulls downward. He skins round and round until he has come to the forelegs, which he skins by pulling the hide off the legs like a stocking—the same way he is pulling the hide off the whole body. He continues on, skinning out the head and being careful about the ears and eyes, until at last the tip of the nose has been removed. The job of removing the hide is then accomplished.

A few points are well worth consideration after you

have removed the pelt. When you sell it, the buyer pays attention to the quality. Every small defect lowers the value in his estimation, and every buyer uses such defects as reasons for paying you less for the skin.

In skinning, don't try to remove all the fat and muscle tissue still clinging to it until you have stretched the hide.

Clean every blood spot by washing and drying the hair. If blood is left close to the skin, it sometimes decomposes enough to cause the hair to slip at that spot. After drying, you can rub some dry sawdust into the fur to remove all moisture. Brush it out.

Wet skins should be dried and combed to bring up all the natural beauty. They won't shrink until the skin itself starts to dry.

Don't wait to stretch the hide until it has dried, or you will have an inferior job. Even if the head end, where the hide is thinnest, dries, you cannot do a respectable job. It may pay to soak the dried end long enough for it to become pliable; then dry it with cloth and sawdust and stretch.

Now comes the task of stretching. There are several ways in vogue. The commonest way is to nail the hide to a flat surface like a barn door or side of a building. If the hide has been removed by the first-mentioned method, it is already open; and it may be tacked up with the head stretched open first. The skin should then be allowed to hang down. A stout tack is inserted at the base of the tail and the skin on the tail opened to the tip with a knife. This should be held open by several tacks. The skin should not be pulled down and stretched lengthwise so hard that there will be too little width to it after it is dried, but should be allowed to hang naturally, and then tacked. After this, the front and rear legs and finally the sides should be pulled out evenly, opening the hide and stretching it as taut as possible. Go over it with the fleshing knife and scrape the surplus fat away so that it may dry quickly. Once it is dry, it may be removed and hung up; it will not shrink. Remove all possible fat so that it will not drip and mess up the other skins in close proximity to it.

If the skin has been removed stocking fashion, it is necessary to slit it down the middle and slit open the front legs before it is tacked in place, if it is to be stretched open, but if you wish to stretch it cased, leave as is.

Some buyers encourage the hunter to place the skin on stretchers such as those on which a muskrat is stretched, with the hair on the inside. Without doubt, a nice job can be done this way, but the skin cannot be turned inside out when dry and must be split down the middle. It is awkward to handle in this way. If the market demands it, however, better satisfy the market.

Some buyers prefer the square skin. Square stretching can be done by using a hoop with thongs, as in primitive times when nails were handmade and scarce; or it may be done in the modern manner of tacking to a wall. We prefer to tack to a wall, but upside down for ease of fleshing.

Stretch as nearly square or rectangular as possible.

Those who have tried and been unable to square a skin have usually forgotten to slit the nose. Make a straight cut through the nose clear down almost to the ears. If you have peeled the hide off stocking fashion, make slits along the belly, the front legs, nose, and tail.

Tack the tip of the tail at the highest point. Tack the base, spread and tack the hind legs, and work the hide into a neat rectangle, as near a square as possible. It is not as difficult as you may think.

Fleshing can be done from tail to head, thus fleshing *with* the hair follicles, not against them.

As a matter of fact, there are two reasons why this matter of stretching is so important. Stretching causes the skin to dry more quickly and makes it easier to handle, and it enables one to get the largest price possible for the skin. The way the skin dries the first time is not an indication of how it will look after it has come through the tanning process. If a skin is stretched incorrectly, the damage can be undone by soaking the skin and restretching it later. After it has been tanned, the furrier soaks it and stretches it any way he wishes to suit his needs. The leather can be stretched after tanning just as well as it can before drying in the first place. So, stretching is more a matter of making a good impression on the trade than it is a matter of width or length. However, in the eyes of the buyer these things count and should be remembered.

Some old-fashioned hunters still stretch the hides by using a sapling bent into a circle or square. They cut small holes in the skin all around the edge and then lash it with a cord to the sapling, threading the cord over the stick, through a hole, then over the stick again until it is pulled out in every direction. Although this method produces good results and keeps the skin clean and taut, it probably does not warrant all the trouble it causes its users.

For years it was the custom to salt all hides in order to preserve them. This is totally unnecessary and tanners discourage it, as it causes them some little trouble in tanning. If the weather is hot and there is danger of spoilage, salt is useful. Its chief action is not so much to kill bacteria as to dry. Salt is a glutton for water; it soaks the water out of the leather and dries the hide, tending to preserve it.

Some hunters make it a practice to stretch their coon hides in the attic where it is very hot in the daytime and cold at night. Such hides seem to dry well without spoiling. Others will dry them in the cellar where the furnace will provide constant heat. Still others, the great majority, will stretch them in the barn, the garage, the woodshed, and, in fact, anywhere that vermin will not molest them.

When the market demands it, casing, or stretching stockinglike, over a board or wire stretcher of the correct size is perhaps the easiest. A fleshing board, approximately three feet long and a foot wide at the base, tapering to a point, is useful. By using a dull draw shave, hoe, or long-bladed knife, the surplus fat can readily be scraped off. Stretchers should be in large, medium, and small sizes. If they are of wood, simply pull the skin down over, flesh side out, and tack the bottom edges, after pulling tight. Wire raccoon stretchers are on the market and are light, durable, and easy to use.

Some hunters and even tannery employees flesh from head to tail. This is not as efficient or as proper a way to proceed as fleshing the opposite way, because the hair follicles are placed in the skin slanting from tail to head. It is better for the ultimate skin to flesh from tail to head; this is in many respects a cleaner job but more difficult to start because of the heavy fat deposits about the hind legs and under the skin near the tail.

Should you fail to sell your hides in the winter and want to keep them until the next season, don't leave them tacked to the barn or garage or hanging on stretchers through warm weather. Take the skins down, remove any surplus fat, and carry them to a cold-storage plant where they can be properly stored. The small expense of keeping your bundle of hides will be worth many times your loss if you fail to store them properly.

Coon cookery. The flesh of the raccoon is considered a table delicacy practically everywhere that the country connoisseur exists. Those who have partaken of rare meats have not as much to say in favor of raccoon meat as have the chief exponents of church suppers. It is doubtful whether these cosmopolites, however, really know much about the taste of coon accompanied by sweet potatoes, white potatoes, turnips, and other adjuncts. Indeed, perhaps here a little confession is in order on the part of the senior author.

He once went hunting with a friend who had received

a commission from a local church to supply the group with five good coons, six if they were small. They hunted nearly a week and the dogs had no luck; it was bitterly cold and no coons seemed to be out. Then came a very warm night two nights before the scheduled date of the supper. They hunted desperately to add four more coons to the two they had taken. They got one, but it was then three o'clock in the morning. They remembered that the dog would hunt skunk, so they hied to a broad meadow and promptly bagged three nice, large, fat skunks. The coon supper was a great success. Probably few persons could actually tell the difference between coon and skunk.

At a coon supper many other meats are added, and everybody goes home happy. One gets very tired of the meat, for no matter what is done to it, it still remains greasy. Coon meat makes a good food for a hard-working man who can stand more fat in his diet than can a man of sedentary habits. As the Southerners say, "It had better," because a great many families have much coon to eat and seem to thrive on it as well as on any meat.

Under the front legs of a racoon there will be found a pair of glands which are said to add a very gamy taste to the coon if they are not removed when the carcass is cooked. Better remove them, but if you do not, no harm will be done. We have tasted coon meat when these glands had not been removed and couldn't tell the difference.

The methods of preparation are varied. Coon can be cooked about like lamb; however, unlike lamb, coon meat has to be parboiled first if the coon is old and if people object to the gamy flavor. Baking soda and vinegar are commonly added to the water in which it is boiled, both for the purpose of removing the gamy flavor, but this is, of course, absurd, because one is an acid and the other alkaline in action; either one or the other should be used. No one has yet said which is proper. Cooks who use neither say that they cannot tell the difference.

The favorite recipe for cooking wild duck is to put a brick in the water with the duck and boil until the brick becomes tender, but no such heroic measure is demanded for coon. If boiled for three hours, even the oldest ones become tender. Following the boiling and the skimming off of the surplus fat collected on the water, roasting is in order. Some cooks prefer to place white potatoes or sweet potatoes sprinkled liberally with brown sugar around the coon, while others use nothing at all. Salt should be sprinkled over the roast which, of course, is stuffed with bread crumbs and giblets or whatever kind of stuffing is in popular demand. The following recipes for cooking raccoon have been tried by us and are excellent:

Recipes for raccoon. The most important factor to remember in cooking a raccoon is to remove as much of the fat as possible before the culinary efforts. It is here that the "gamy taste," so objectionable to many, is found.

Three parboilings are necessary. In the first, the raccoon is covered with cold water, brought to a boil, and then this water is discarded. The second follows the same procedure with the addition of one tablespoonful of black pepper and one tablespoonful of baking soda. In the third barpoiling, clear water is again used. The raccoon is then ready for roasting, boiling, frying, or whatever method is desired. Since the meat, when cooked, is very similar to leg of lamb or chicken, any method of cooking these meats may be used.

The usual procedure is to stuff the raccoon with a poultry or other favorite dressing and then to roast at 325 degrees for 2½ hours. Some cooks claim a great deal of success and probably more acceptance when the raccoon is cut up prior to roasting.

The leftover meat may be cubed, with celery, green pepper, hard-boiled egg, and chopped parsley added to make a delicious salad when mixed with mayonnaise.

Another successful method of using up the leftovers is to mix a can of condensed mushroom soup, one can of green peas, and a small amount of grated cheese to the meat and to bake for about 45 minutes at 350 degrees.

A delicious meatloaf may be made by cutting the meat off the bones and grinding it up. Add ½ cup cracker crumbs, ½ cup ground onion, 1⅓ tbsp. salt, ½ tsp. pepper, 2 eggs, ¼ tsp. thyme, and one cup evaporated milk. Place in a meatloaf pan set in a pan of hot water and bake in a moderate oven (350 degrees) for 1¾ hours.

As an accompaniment to the above dishes, sweet potatoes or yams seem to be universally accepted as *the* dish. A tossed green salad and any favorite dessert will help to complete the "Hunter's Special."

The stuffed coon should be roasted until it is nicely browned all over, and it should occasionally be basted. The juices in the bottom of the pan can be made into gravy, thickened to the desired consistency with flour and salted to taste.

In some homes coon meat is also boiled and served with rice, just as is lamb. This is said to be very delicious. The rice absorbs any surplus fat. The meat is taken off the bones when served in this manner. It is sometimes stewed and served with vegetables, again after the manner of lamb. It can also be fricasseed, as chicken, or served fried, Maryland style. Many people prefer it the last way, and it does indeed have some advantages from an esthetic point of view.

Few people like to see the carcass served on the table; it brings back memories especially to the poor fellow who dressed it. It is not a bad idea to dismember the carcass in the kitchen. At every coon supper where someone carves, there will be remarks about how much the coon looks like a cat or a monkey, and inquisitive Johnny will ask if Daddy is sure it is not a skunk. If our experience is worth anything, it indicates that when the coon is served in pieces on a platter and camouflaged as much as possible, it will be all for the best, because someone is sure to bite on a BB shot anyway, and that will start the conversation back to the coon hunt and what a good time everybody had. Then Bill will tell how the dogs stretched the coon, and Mike will describe how the coon squealed, and as sure as shooting someone will have to get up and leave the table.

We should try to make the occasion of eating coon meat, which is really very delectable, as pleasant as possible, remembering that we do not describe the slaughter house every time we have lamb for Sunday dinner.

12. *Coon-Dog Field Trials*

SIX BAYING HOUNDS are lined up at the starting line, each dog held securely by his trainer. A crowd of eager men and not a few women gather about them in a great horseshoe. The starter tolls off the words, "On your marks, get set," and blows a whistle. Away they fly in a pack, rushing madly along a trail that has been previously laid by a man dragging a sack filled with debris from a raccoon's nest. The crowd watches intently and as soon as the hounds have disappeared over the hill and into the brush moves as quickly as possible off to its right a quarter of a mile and gathers in another horseshoe about a group of trees.

A rope, supported in part by several stakes, has been placed from one tree to another; and no one in the crowd may go nearer to the tree than the rope. Within the semicircular area encompassed by the rope stand nine men—six dog handlers and three judges. Two flags on short poles have been placed 150 feet from the tree; behind each flag stands another judge. Another flag has also been placed just twenty-five paces from each side of the line.

The dogs are running the final heat. They have been elected by elimination heats from a field of ninety-six coonhounds. This heat covers a distance of four miles, giving the crowd time to see both the start and the finish. No one wants to miss a movement of the dogs. All is very still. Only the friends of the coon hunters are whispering in subdued voices. The real hunters have learned from long experience in the woods at night to maintain a deathly stillness while listening for their dogs.

Up in the tree, chained there for security's sake, sits a coon on a limb. By looking closely, anyone in the crowd can see its movements; and many spend the time watching it as they wait to hear the first faint baying. Many have placed bets on the winning dog. Others have made mental wagers too, and everyone has a favorite. A few have even taken the trouble to time the elimination heats and have pretty well decided in advance which dog will be the winner.

After much ear straining, the listeners catch the baying. Before they know it, in through the field gallops a lithe tan figure, running as gracefully and lightly as a deer as he follows the unseen trail. Then behind him appears another, this time a large black-and-tan with a great bass voice. He is fast, but he lumbers as he runs. A third comes dashing in with his head high off the ground, and the crowd wonders why he is not in the lead. Behind them come the other three.

Straight between the flags romps the little tan dog, straight for the group of trees. He is almost flying compared to the gait of most ordinary hounds. He goes by; he has lost the trail. Then he wheels and turns. The big black-and-tan goes by too. He sees the tan dog turn and he turns, but too late. The third dog has been watching everything, including the actions of the leaders. He is an oldtimer. He knows from long experience that the tree is the one in the center of the horseshoe of people. He doesn't even stop to smell up the other trees, but, with a great running jump, he bounds up the right tree, barking as he does so. Less than a second after him the big black-and-tan lets out his first tree bark.

The handlers rush to their dogs to stave off fights, putting their leashes on and rewarding them with much petting and many cheering words.

A large purse has been won by the dog which barked tree first, but the others have also won sizeable purses by virtue of winning their heats. The second dog receives a goodly slice of the final-heat prize money.

Following this event is the line final. In some coonhound field trials the line final precedes the tree final. From each heat a tree dog and a line dog have been chosen. Any kind of fast hound has a good chance to win the line final. One finds ringers from foxhound kennels and mongrels of all sorts competing for the line prize. Dogs that have no more right to be called coon-hounds than Pomeranians may win this prize, although more often than not the prize is won by a straight cooner. Often, too, the same dog wins both line and tree final. It adds just that much more zest to the events and helps swell the crowd, as well as the number of entries in the meet.

Let us point out here that we are talking about field trials and field-trial dogs. This is more or less a new sport. Field trials have no more relation to real night coon hunting than the drag foxhunt of society folks has to the New England variety of foxhunting, where the lone hunter slings his gun over his arm and sallies forth to sit and wait for his hound to strike the fox track and run it. Occasionally the bona fide coon hunter pooh-poohs the field trial, but should he? Coonhound field trials admittedly do not test the worth of a real cooner. The dog that wins a field trial may be a fast foxhound that, taken into the woods at night, would run the first fox whose trail he could find and forget all about coons. Or he might be a deer dog. In fact, it is a safe thing to say that coonhound field-trial winners are generally not coon dogs at all, but simply fast hounds that have been trained and selected for their ability to follow a trail quickly to a tree, in which they can usually smell or see a coon, and bark. There are exceptions to this, but they are indeed rare. There is excitement for any dog who is entered. Dogs strain at their leashes, bay, bark, and start off quickly in a rush that peps any dog up to do things that he wouldn't usually do, just as deer-broken dogs will often join their companions in running a deer, when they would never do so alone.

Be this as it may, there are many good things that can be said for the field trial—so many, in fact, that its extension should be urged and all coon hunters would do well to engage in it. We believe that there is not only a place for it, but that it does a great deal of good both for coonhounds and for their owners. We admit that field-trial dogs are seldom great night dogs and that trailing a bag of wet nest material is not the same as trailing an experienced old ringtail through swamp and briar patch, over ledges and fallen logs; but that does not in the least minimize the value of the field trial. It is certain that these trials will not harm a good coon dog. There are, in fact, some good dogs that are stimulated to do better work in packs than they ever do alone. Once in a while, however, one finds an experienced coon dog that will not run in a coon trial when a man's scent is alongside it.

The coonhound field trial has come to stay. Enthusiasts are breeding dogs that are especially suited to that particular job, without necessarily considering their night-hunting ability. Today in many states the coonhound field trials outnumber field trials of any other variety.

Moreover, there is coming to be a standard procedure for the events. Rules are becoming uniform. The distances run are getting more and more to be very nearly a mile for elimination heats. It has been found that the same course may be followed in one heat after another. It is necessary to change the course only in the final heat. The dogs are becoming more uniform. We can remember seeing a motley crew of mutts assembled for these trials several years ago—German shepherds, Airedales, Doberman pinschers, setters, a pointer, and hounds ranging in size all the way from little beagles up to dogs almost as large as bloodhounds. Sometimes a nonhound would win too, but not very often.

The tree dog to be used in coonhound field trials must have speed, giving him a chance to win the line final, and a highly developed treeing aptitude. The dog that has so far evolved from this gradual selection seems to be between a greyhound and whippet in size, almost as slimly built as a whippet, and appearing so partly because he is trained down to a little more than skin, muscle, and bones. He usually has medium-length ears. The kind of voice he has doesn't matter in the least because, according to the rules, all he has to do is emit a yodel of any sort and show he knows the right tree.

Sometimes clubs staging their first field trial and still more or less unacquainted with the usual procedure will put on a far better show than those accustomed to these events. In Vermont in the fall of 1934, they had a field trial of this sort which brought shouts of enthusiasm and tears of joy. It was won by old Bob, a dog the senior author had trained. He was a real night dog. The club members of the Vermont Coonhunters' Association, about the finest group of sportsmen it has ever been our pleasure to know, arranged it to be as nearly like a real coon hunt as they possibly could.

They kept the crowd up on a bank overlooking a great meadow and transplanted a sizeable tree which would be in fine view of the audience. They made the long trails with a live coon led through swamps and in all kinds of zigzag paths, much as a coon would travel when he is in the woods. In fact, the only difference was that a man's trail went parallel to the coon's, and the hunt was held in the daylight. Over 100 dogs competed.

Lots of upsets occurred. Many of the professional field-trial men didn't stand a chance in this kind of hunting. All the elimination heats were run, and it was time for the final. The day was hot, and the trailing was very hard, as the trail was over an hour old.

The dogs started, and the crowd watched them make one mistake after another. Finally old Bob with his bob-tail shaking back and forth came along well in advance of the other dogs. Competitors would rush past and lead him for a while, but then he would again forge ahead. He smelled up each tree that the coon had touched, giving a little more excitement to his baying. At this, the less certain cooners would stay and bark up as if the coon were still there. Then Bob would circle and find the trail going away from the tree, and the others would follow. After the hardest kind of work, he finally came to the right tree, made his circle, stayed there, and barked. They say it was one of the finest pieces of work that has been seen by coon hunters in many a year.

Although that wasn't a regular coonhound field trial, you can see why the really fine night dog is handicapped in an ordinary field trial and why the field-trial dog is not so good at night. A good night dog should not "bark up the wrong tree." That is where the expression came from, in fact, for coon hunting has always been of interest to rural America. In order not to bark up the wrong tree, the coon dog of experience will generally circle the tree before he sits down and tells the world that there is a coon up in that particular tree. But if he does that in a field trial, he is out. He might as well give a few barks up the first tree he comes to. We know a lot of the boys in this game of sport, many of whom own winners; but they have often confided to us that their dogs are worthless as night hunters.

Speaking of judging, it is not half as easy as the onlookers seem to think. Each judge writes his choice on a piece of paper and hands it to the head judge. They are closer to the tree than the crowd, and sometimes it is funny to hear the crowd bellow when they have rendered a decision which is absolutely just.

Many recall the murmurs which went up from both sides of the gallery when we were judging the final heat of the Connecticut Championship. That portion of the gallery which was behind the tree never said a word, but those to the right and those to the left booed and had much to say. The reason was simple. The two dogs that came to the tree first barked up on opposite sides.

There was just a split second separating the two barks, and we judges could see both dogs. The tree was so large that a person on one side couldn't see the dog on the other. Naturally, therefore, each group was cheering for the dog that it could see.

There are times, of course, when the judges are wrong and the crowd is right; but the decision of the judges is final and the crowd cannot have a say officially, even though they have much to say unofficially.

Take the case of a field trial in which the final tree was placed right at the bottom of a small hill. The senior author was one of the crowd that day. There was a large entry and the preliminaries had to be run with eight dogs to the heat. We were all gathered about the tree, as is customary, and could hear the dogs coming closer and closer. Over the hilltop they burst, practically in a pack. There was one big red dog, a cross of bloodhound and Irish setter, among the first three. When they were halfway down the hill, this big fellow stopped abruptly and sat down, waited only a moment, and began to bark vociferously. All the others dashed by him and soon were around the tree. The judges' eyes were glued to them only. But the red dog was barking up as surely as a dog could, and what was more, he had been hunting with his eyes as well as his nose, an aptitude he had inherited from his setter parent. He had seen the coon clearly and should have won, by any just decision, according to any rules. But the judges didn't even see him, whereas the crowd saw him plainly and let it be known. In fact, when they saw him bark, many started to walk away because they felt they knew which dog had won. Judging is beset by many opportunities for bad decision and many opportunities where experience as a coon hunter is most desirable.

It often happens that the men planning the field trial choose a tree which is one of a clump of trees. We have seen this happen on several occasions. When the trees are too close together, the night dog has a better chance to win than the trained field-trial dog. The latter will usually rush to the first tree he sees, whereas the former will sniff up several until he has made sure which is the right one. And even then he may stand with his front feet against a nearby tree and bark up because it is the habit of many good night dogs to bark up when they are standing some distance from the tree in which they know the coon to be.

Once we saw a dog win a field trial because the judges knew their business. Less experienced judges would have decided differently. The dog sniffed up several trees and found the right one. He took a long while to give his first bark and when he did, he stood with his feet against a tree fifteen feet away from the correct one. With his head turned in the right direction—toward the proper tree—he let out a series of those noises which we coon hunters call music. He won, and rightly so.

Speaking of the trained field-trial dog, one year two of our friends had the job of laying the trail for the final. They chose a course which was fair to both field-trial and night dogs; but, in coming into the home stretch, they saw a beautiful big tree about a hundred yards from the tree chosen as the final goal. They headed straight for this big tree, but dragged the bag past its base. Then they dragged the bag past still another tree in line with the final one and thence to the final tree.

Having seen this and wanting to watch what would happen, we slipped away from the crowd and hid in some bushes. The dogs came along. The first was a little tan fellow not much larger than a whippet, all but flying. As soon as he found the trail heading straight for a big tree, he came on and with a beautiful leap landed against its trunk and jumped backward, only to leap up barking again and again. Pretty soon, however, he decided that it wasn't the right tree. He had some tree sense, even though he had been trained for field-trial work. He left the other two and ran along the trail. But up the next tree he leaped as ardently as he had the first. Then a heavily built hound trailed past him, after giving only a sniff that told him the coon had not ascended the tree. The tan wisp saw him go and soon overtook him. Of course, he bounded up the final tree, too, with a beautiful flourish, and won. But to us, it seemed a counterpart of the famous hare and tortoise race with the wrong ending. The old night dog should have won that race.

We believe that, in order to bring about a fair competition, the proponents of this very rapidly growing sport of coonhound field trials must decide definitely, once and for all, whether they want to make their competitions real tests for bona fide night dogs or whether they want to make them competitions for genuine field-trial dogs, with all the dramatic possibilities and splendid opportunities for the building of a new kind of thriller for the public as well as for the coon hunter. Personally, we believe that the right thing to do is to run both kinds of meets. The former type is worth while even if for no other reason than for training coon dogs, but this has very limited possibilities. We know that a coon dog will operate as well in the daytime as at night. A smaller number of persons will attend such meets, but it should always be specified that the trial is to be for night dogs. Otherwise it would not be fair to the strictly field-trial type of dog.

One of the nicest features of the coonhound field trial is the opportunity it provides for the whole family to share in the fun. The trials take most of the day, and naturally mother and the children like to come along and bring lunch. The family has frequently had a hand in the training of the dogs, and consequently there are more than a few persons interested in the success of the event. One will see picnic parties all about the grounds at lunch time. The big tent with the cafeteria is always well patronized. The tables under the trees are filled with hungry men, women, and children. Dogs will be tied to trees close to the picnickers, just members of the family. The sociability of the affair adds just that much more to the value of the event in the sporting world.

We see in the genuine specialized coonhound field trial the possibilities of something more engaging and worth while than the greyhound race and something far more thrilling for the public to watch. It is possible by good management to select country in which the course laid will be visible to the audience. They can follow the dogs with their eyes for a mile and see a real race, in contrast to the sprint of the greyhound. At the end they can see the behavior of the dogs at the tree, and this adds a greater factor of chance.

As for the dogs, there never has been any real attempt made, so far as we can learn, to breed a trail hound that is really fast. In fox hunting, the very fast hound drives the fox into its hole and thus is not of much use for sport. The sight hounds have been made for speed, and they have it. But they are of no use in following a trail by scent. Someday, someone is going to combine the speed of the sight hound with the desire and ability to trail that we find in our best scent hounds. We shall then have hounds for field trials which can pass any which are competing today, just as a modern speedboat can pass a boat propelled with oars.

May the day soon come when the sponsors of the coonhound field trial realize the wonderful possibilities inherent in their sport and make plans to lay their courses in such a way that a great number of onlookers, who may not be coon hunters themselves, may enjoy them. As surely as they do this, the sport is going to flourish in a greater way than ever dreamed. Today the coonhound clubs are hiding their lights under bushels. Tomorrow they will find themselves in a sport so popular that thousands of persons who love dogs can enjoy and profit by the development of the sport's tremendous potentialities.

13. *How to Conduct a Field Trial*

FIELD TRIALS have now been held for a sufficient number of years for a fairly uniform program to have been set up. The ideal, of course, which may eventually come about, will be worked as follows: Every local association will hold its trial on dates set by the state association that is the larger representative of the several locals. When the best two line dogs and the best two tree dogs have been selected from each club, the local as a club will pay for sending or taking the winners to the state trials, at which will be gathered the best dogs from all the local clubs. The winners of the state trials will then be selected and two line dogs and two tree dogs chosen to represent the state at the nationals.

As the situation is at present, any group might announce that it is going to hold the national championships; and, if it is sufficiently powerful, it can attract dogs from five hundred miles away. With a great burst of ballyhoo, the group announces the national champion and publishes his picture in the sporting magazines. This has been done, but it actually means nothing except many extra dollars for the group that sponsored the "racket."

To declare that a dog is national champion should mean something. Only proper organization can help to achieve that condition. Even then, it is doubtful if the winner should be declared to be the best dog in the United States. All that can be said is that, of the dogs competing, a certain dog won.

The club or association which undertakes to conduct a field trial takes a responsibility on its shoulders which unfortunately too many of them accept lightly. Conducting a worth-while field trial is a man's job, and it would pay the clubs to employ a manager who knew the business, just as the great dog-show associations employ an experienced person to manage their affairs. Having attended many field trials, we should like to present for consideration the following suggestions, each of which has been carried out at successful field trials in one form or another. They will be found useful under nearly all conditions.

A field trial, in order to be most successful, should be as dramatic as possible. Holding a local event in some farmer's back yard is one thing, but holding a statewide or interstate affair to which men are invited from long distances is quite another. Even the local event, if it is properly managed, can be such a drawing card that hundreds of persons will attend.

Remember that in every center of population there are possibly thousands who have at one time or another gone on a coon hunt. Indeed, coon hunts have been dramatized in many a book and motion picture, and all kinds of people have seen such pictures and read such books and would like to see a version of the real thing. Suppose that your club holds an event, inviting the general public, and no provision has been made for viewing the trials—they are started and finished up near a swamp, and the public has to stand in swamp grass and fret. Suppose that there is little opportunity to see the hounds; suppose the trials are not run off on time and that there is argument between the judges and the men leading the coons or dragging the bag. Suppose there is not an adequate place to be used as a toilet. Suppose many things! Under such conditions, can you expect the public to come and see your field trial next year? Will even the wives of the contestants, after standing all day, come again? No, indeed.

First, thorough preparation and planning must precede every trial, and that should be based upon what others have found to be helpful from experience.

The Ballyhoo. One of the most important things to remember is the ballyhoo; it is the basis upon which the success of the meet depends. The more entries one obtains, the larger the purses can be and the greater the interest. Contestants will come from great distances; professionals will bring their dogs. There is no reason why the professionals should detract from the local interest. Judges can qualify all dogs in order of finishing, and not only can a grand final be run but a final for all local dogs as well.

A committee should be appointed to take care of publicity. The task of this committee should be not only to work up general public enthusiasm but also to act as a steering committee to keep up the highest standard at the field trial. Remember the attitude of the public. There will be as many interested spectators as there will be owners of dogs. These men and women will be persons who "used to own the best coon dog in America. He could tree a coon when. . . ." There will be many who just love a hound-dog. There will be some who love the hounds' voices and others, those who go to races of all kinds, who get tremendous excitement from just watching the race. They'll all be there, and the committee must cater to each class, if the meet is to be a success.

We suggest that the advertising be along the lines of general local interest, but newspaper articles such as any experienced newspaper man knows how to get published and distributed over the AP and UP wires must have more than local interest. If nothing better is found to catch the editor's eye, write an invitation to the Governor, telling him that many meritorious citizens are going to attend, and get a picture of the Governor (who may have once hunted coons) talking to the oldest coon hunter in the state. Perchance you can find something more doggy, such as showing the picture of some famous dog who once saved a boy's life or treed fifty coons in a season, or a picture of the country's supposed champion coon dog, which is expected to attend. Here and there through the campaign, sprinkle in a picture of the Game Commissioner, the Superintendent of Fish and Game, and half a dozen well-known names; and let the public know that they will be present. Newspapers can't resist dog news if it is sufficiently well dressed, and you need have no fear of reaching many people if the man at the head has ideas.

Magazine news is different. Of course, there are lists for coming sporting events in several, and these should include notices of the field trial. If the club is able to afford it, printed advertisements can be placed in magazines well in advance of the meet. Remember that most of them come out close to the middle of the month before the date mark. Mention in the advertisements that details will be sent to persons desiring to enter dogs, so that it is known in advance how many dogs must be accommodated.

The next usual step is to send individual postcards or letters with details of the meet and application blanks. Postcards should be printed and not mimeographed, as the latter often become blurred and leave less space for the return information.

Always tell how to reach the place where the trial is to be held. Arrows which point the way are good and necessary, but sometimes wind, rain, and mischievous boys remove them. So let strangers know how to find their way by printing a small map, if possible.

Printed programs can be issued giving the numbers of the dogs if the club decides to have a closed meet (that is, with the entries closing by a certain date). This is a wise precaution, because it helps to estimate the number of dogs and allows time for making plans. Today, however, the majority of the meets are open. The time limit for entries is generally set as the starting time of the meet or possibly two hours afterward. This is both a good and bad practice. It encourages a larger entry, but it discourages promptness; and, when a flood of entries comes in late, it may necessitate running much larger heats in order to finish in time. Many participants go home disgusted and vow never to come again. Of course, the club can estimate the number of entries by the number that came the previous year, if the club has had experience. It is the first year's attempt and the activities of the publicity committee that make possible such estimates.

The other part of the committee's work is the grounds arrangement. All of the interested persons certainly would like to see the dogs. Practically no field trials afford sufficient opportunity for this. Most field trials in the past have been equivalent to holding a dog show and allowing the public to see only the show ring. The public wants to see the dogs. So let them!

Since it is difficult to obtain regular benches, a lot of strong stakes can be procured—have points sharpened on them and drive them into the ground in two rows.

Each dog is tied to a stake with a chain. The owner is then requested to leave the dog alone except when necessary to exercise him. The stakes should be at least two by two and set at least fifty feet apart, so that it will be possible to stretch ropes in front of the stakes to provide a causeway in which the spectators can walk and inspect the dogs. They must be warned to stay outside the ropes by signs and watchmen. If there are a hundred dogs entered, fifty on each side will make a very sizable row of dogs and add tremendously to the ballyhoo. You should get the air of carnival into the procedure—"jazz it up" so the public will feel they are getting their money's worth.

The Ground Arrangement. There are several things necessary in the ground equipment that must not be overlooked. These are:

1. A large tent, to which the public can retire in case of rain. In one end of this it is well to sell a concession so that a little sum may be added to the treasury to help defray expenses. At the other end, there should be a large book and attached pencil on a table with someone standing nearby urging all visitors to register by name and address.

2. An admission gate, if possible. Some clubs prefer not to charge admission, but 50 cents or a dollar is easy to get from the public; and, if the proper plans have been carried out and permission obtained from the owner of the property, it is not so difficult to restrict the meet to paid admissions. Be sure to have tickets printed and to give receipts to the customers, so they may be checked

on in case it becomes apparent that too many are entering the grounds as unpaid guests.

3. Lavatories. These may be of tent material or temporary houses.

4. A great deal of rope and many stakes. This is necessary to rope off the crowd and place in front of the rows of dogs.

5. Four flagpoles to be used for the trials, two at a time. One set is in use while the other is being placed for the next heat.

6. Spaces to throw rubbish.

7. Signs. There should be one each for the following:

ADMISSION GATE	HANDS OFF DOGS (four such
THIS WAY TO DOGS	signs)
MEN'S TOILET	TO FIELD TRIALS (four such
WOMEN'S TOILET	signs)

8. Fifty signs with arrows may be placed along the roadsides pointing to the place where the meet is to be held. Half of these should have the arrows pointed in one direction and half in the other, as there is a difference on which side of the road the sign is placed. The signs should be in waterproof ink and printed in as large type, within reason, as the printer has. Be sure they contain the essential information, displaying most prominently the most important item:

COONHOUND FIELD TRIALS

Hadley, Ohio   *October 30, 1952*

9. A large blackboard for displaying announcements of dogs' numbers and winners.

The exact arrangement of the grounds is determined by the locality. The best possible location is a hill on which the crowd may stand and see in all directions. If the hill has trees around it, but not on the very top, it is ideal. Thus the trail may be laid beginning at a point where the crowd can see down into the valley, and back toward the top of the hill to the tree. The crowd can thus see far away down the hill, watch the actions of the dogs, and see them come up the hill to the end. There are several such hills in nearly every county in the United States that has any hill at all. The prairie states are not too good in this respect. But even on a prairie, provided there are trees, the crowd can be held in check.

Many field trials are now run over trails which the public cannot see, except for the finish, the dogs being taken to the start in a truck.

We cannot overemphasize the need for dressing the meet with all the show and carnival atmosphere possible. A few state game wardens will help. People will respect the club more if they understand that they must abide by the rules. To this end it is well to hand each person coming into the grounds a printed or mimeographed copy of ground rules and ask them in the name of good sportsmanship to read and abide by them.

The Field Trial Proper. The day of the trial has arrived. It is held rain or shine, of course. It starts at nine or ten o'clock. The judges arrive an hour ahead of time, consult, look over the grounds, and decide where the trails shall be laid, after estimating possible number of entries.

By half an hour beforehand, the first trail has been laid. It will probably be made by dragging a bag filled with coon-pen debris and dung which has been soaked in water. At the end, in a tree designated by the judges, a live raccoon is tied, after having been passed up to the man climbing the tree. Sometimes the coon is in a wire box, if the tree is high enough to allow the box to be hidden by leaves. But it is better for the dogs to have the coon placed twenty feet up where he may be seen every time. This is better, because some of the better coon dogs entered, if they are experienced, will have learned never to bark tree until they have done some investigating to see that the trail surely ends at that tree. If they see the coon, they will bark without further investigating. Many a dog has been cheated from a prize because he used his head, where a stupid dog simply ran to the tree and barked. Such a dog as the latter would frequently be barking up the wrong tree if used in the woods.

The use of a "scent-stick" is coming more and more into vogue. Many field trial associations use it exclusively.

There is no harm in dragging a bag. Even when a smart dog wouldn't follow it in the woods if by himself, the excitement of the occasion and other dogs will cause him to chase along as well as though it were the trail of a real coon. The chief disadvantage is that the trail left by the bag produces such a strong odor that a dog can follow it from some distance away, whereas if the trail were laid by a coon, the dog would have to keep close to the trail. The club will have to debate this issue. It will also have to debate the issue of how old the trail should be. Most field trials see that one trail is being laid while the last is being run. The day has a great deal to do with it. Hot dry days make it difficult to follow any trail, while wet days make it easy to follow even old ones. Some clubs alternate, using first a coon, then a bag, provided they use the same trail and tree for each heat. In some states, Humane Societies prohibit the use of live coons for trail laying.

Crossing the Trail. It has often been suggested that in the grand final a very long and a very old trail be laid and that the trail be crossed by several animals, each of which is fresher than the coon track. This would do much to weed out the coon dogs from the ordinary ringers. A pair of rabbits, foxes, or a deer could be led across the trail. If no deer is available, a goat will sometimes do. A dog that ran any of these trails would be at once disqualified if he went more than 100 feet. This limit is placed to allow dogs which are led off by dogs ahead of them to return to the trail. Such a field trial is not only worth while but almost necessary to separate the field-trial dogs from the coon dogs. When the ideal coon dog is approached in breeding, such tests will be necessary.

Each dog will have a number painted on his side by the numbering committee. This committee will also have charge of drawing the numbers to arrange the dogs in heats. Some discretion must be used by them to see that only one dog from each owner is entered. Thus, if a man enters four dogs, the committee must see to it that only one should be run in a heat. This is done by athletic committees in arranging the heats for runners at athletic meets and can be done for a coonhound field trial.

A man with a megaphone should be stationed between the crowd and the tree, out of the line of vision, and as soon as the heat has been decided, the judges should tell this announcer, who should then announce the result to the crowd. He should tell the number of the dog and the owner's name, putting all the fervor into the act that Joe Humphries used to put into announcing the winner of a prize fight.

On the blackboard, the numbers of the dogs in the heats are posted. In ample time before the heat, the announcer should call off the numbers of the dogs and their owners' names. The owners who are not actually attending the dogs in another heat should be with the crowd, according to the rules.

It should be permissible to allow the owner to take his dog half an hour before the heat starts and lead him in an exercising section. Many a field trial has been lost by an excellent dog having to stop and urinate or defecate during the running of the trial. Every wise owner will give his dog plenty of time before the race.

After every trial there will be a discussion as to which really was the best dog. There will always be excuses, and for that reason the free-for-all is now a fixture of nearly every trial and should be in every one. This should be a long race, at least a mile long; and a nice trophy should be allowed for the winner, both a line trophy and a tree trophy.

There will always be a group which wants to bet; some will argue as to which has the better dog, and generally there will be what is commonly called a "pot race." The men chip in a designated amount and hire the man who lays the trail to lay a trail for their dogs. They then hold a race, if the judges are not tired and ready to go home. The winner gets all the money that has been put into the pot. After this, the curtain falls upon the field trial, so far as the public is concerned. Not so for the members of the club.

Now comes the cleaning up. The club should not be satisfied until the members have thoroughly cleaned the grounds. This means burning all papers, being positive that no bottles are left around where animals may be cut or where the glass may be plowed under. The latter may injure men weeding later or cut the bare feet of boys or the feet of animals. This is just as much an essential of a field trial as any other feature because, unless it is done, the location will not be loaned for another season. Once a location has been chosen, the public comes to know it and it is well to hold the event there each following season.

Nor is the work over for the publicity committee. Usually there will be reporters handy to tell the readers of their papers who won. A short notice should be given, however, to the press associations, detailing every bit of interesting information and listing all the notables who attended (because names make news). If the Governor did attend, be sure to have his picture petting the winning dog in the next Sunday special editions of all the leading state papers. This is part of next year's publicity.

14. *Standard Field Trial Runs*

MOST OF THE COONHOUND field trials are run under the rules formulated from experience by the National Coon Dog Field Trial Association. These are the rules under which the Leafy Oak Trials are run. Rightly or wrongly this great event has come to be thought of as the United States Championship. It has attracted many of the best dogs of the country and the prizes have been high. The members of the N.C.D.F.T.A. deserve only praise for their excellent management and for the rules which they have given to the rest of the associations.

NATIONAL COON DOG FIELD TRIAL
ASSOCIATION RULES FOR 1951

Rule No. 1. The rules as set forth herein must be complied with by all members and promoters of the N.C.D.F.T.A. and by all members and promoters of the various field-trial circuits that have adopted these rules, and upon violation, after having a written charge filed against them by any member, is subject to being expelled or fined upon a hearing by the Board of Directors in whose circuit they are a member of.

Rule No. 2. All dogs admitted to grounds are subject to a physical examination by a licensed veterinarian, and in such cases where dogs may be showing symptoms of suffering from a contagious disease, or being otherwise unfit to enter open competition, such dogs must be removed from grounds, clear of contact with all other dogs.

Rule No. 3. Any person or dog owner creating a disturbance, persistent and repeated altercations with the Judges over decisions, use of profanity or other improper language, intoxicated or abusive shall be put off the grounds and his dogs disqualified.

Rule No. 4. A drag shall be composed of a club-size coon-grease scent stick that is made by widely advertised scent dealers.

Rule No. 5. A coon will be placed high up in the Judge tree in elimination heats and shall there remain during the trial, and shall be concealed as much as possible with natural foliage. If requested by dog owners a coon must be placed in semifinal and final tree in the same manner.

Rule No. 6. If possible, line Judges must be where they can be seen by the tree Judges at all times.

Rule No. 7. All dogs to qualify for line or tree must pass between line flags going in direction of home tree. Line flags to be spaced approximately one hundred and fifty (150) feet apart.

Rule No. 8. Any number of dogs may be nominated by one proven owner or no more than six Senior and six Junior dogs from a combination of owners. Entries will not be accepted from a combination of more than two owners. No entries accepted by Kennel name. Nine dogs may be nominated by a combination of not more than two owners when running for a separate Junior or Senior Final.

Rule No. 9. (a) Where entries are nominated, any entrant having more dogs than the number of heats will be compelled to run as per-ratio two or more per each.

(b) If nominations are not required, any entrant entering more dogs than number of heats to be run shall be given the right to withdraw extra dogs before any heats are drawn and entry fee shall be refunded. If entrant elects not to withdraw extra dogs they shall run as drawn.

(c) Any entrant having more qualifications than the number of semifinal heats will be compelled to run as per-ratio, two or more dogs per each. All dogs qualifying for semifinal must be drawn to semifinal heats and run in semifinal drawn to. Semifinal drawings must be made in public.

Rule No. 10. The name, sex and color of each entrant must accompany each nomination together with the name and address of owner or nominator.

Rule No. 11. The management reserves the right, by refunding entry fee, to bar and prohibit any dog or dogs entered, when owners, trainer or agent has wilfully entered his dog or dogs under assumed name.

Rule No. 12. All dogs must be entered under their rightful racing names and there shall be no substitution of dogs.

Rule No. 13. No re-entries will be accepted.

Rule No. 14. The Management assumes no responsibility in relation to conditions which may arise due to negligence or tardiness of any owner or attendant to bring his dog to starting post or auction block, after his or her name and number has been called. Neither will the Management be responsible for conduct or safety of any dog or individual.

Rule No. 15. All elimination heats will be contested over one route.

Rule No. 16. Ordinarily, elimination, semifinal and final heats will consist of not over ten dogs.

Rule No. 17. In no event will any elimination heat be run over.

Rule No. 18. In no event will any division of semifinal be contested over unless all the divisions fail to produce a winner.

Rule No. 19. Elimination, semifinal, and final heats shall be run until darkness intervenes, but in no event will be started after darkness unless owners or trainers of dogs participating in such heats by a majority consent request Management to run such heats.

Rule No. 20. No owner or attendant will be permitted to train or exercise his or her dog over course as has been adopted by Management for elimination, semifinal or grand final heats. Failure to recognize this rule automatically disqualifies said dogs. Management shall keep from revealing courses as much as possible until time for trail to be laid.

Rule No. 21. All dogs and attendants after having assembled at starting post shall become in charge of starting Judge under whose jurisdiction they shall remain until signal has been given.

Rule No. 22. Starter Judges shall drop a wooden object, plainly visible to all dog handlers at the start of each heat.

Rule No. 23. Any dog which in any manner or cause may become liberated at source of trail or is not released at the time the starter has given the signal to the entire field, shall automatically become disqualified and shall not be entitled to any consideration by official Judges unless permission is granted by starter or released at second signal, and in such cases all starting fees are forfeited by owner or attendant. If dog or dogs are encouraged in any way or any part of trail after their release at starting line, they will be disqualified.

Rule No. 24. (a) No owner or attendant or spectator shall be permitted during process of any heat to approach within thirty feet of specified trail or home tree until Judges have designated by blowing whistle that a decision has been reached.

(b) In case a dog is handled at the tree without permission of Judge or Field Marshal, said dog shall be disqualified.

(c) In the event dogs become involved or locked in fight at tree no further consideration shall be given to said dogs by the official Judges unless they separate immediately.

Rule No. 25. Any owner or attendant who may call in or leash his dog or show or shout encouragement to his dog without permission of the Field Marshal before Judges have designated by blowing whistle that decision has been rendered, automatically causes his dog to become disqualified by the Field Marshal from winning any part of the heat (tree, line, or second line).

Rule No. 26. Any dog may win both tree and line heat money and both first tree and first line winner will be eligible to enter semifinal or Finals.

Rule No. 27. All dogs to qualify for either line or tree must be retained at the tree until the Judges' decisions are received by the Field Marshal.

Rule No. 28. In no event will a semifinal heat be contested over the same course as has been used in any elimination heat. Neither will any Grand Final be contested over a course used in elimination or semifinal.

Rule No. 29. Five minutes are to be given, after first dog passes through line flags going in direction of home tree, to qualify for all the money in elimination heats and semifinals. Ten minutes shall be given in Finals. In the event no dog qualifies at the line after 15 minutes from time released at starting post in heats or semifinals the heat or semifinal will be declared dead. Thirty minutes will be allowed in Finals, and if no qualification then the Final will be run over until winner declared under conditions of rules. In the event no dog trees in Finals within the limit of time, the first dog having qualified at line shall receive first tree money and second dog shall receive second tree money. In the event only one dog qualifies that dog shall receive entire tree money. One dog can win both tree and line money in the Grand Final.

Rule No. 30. Purses and trails are subject to Management of their respective trials.

Rule No. 31. All dogs participating must be hauled to starting post by conveyance furnished by Management unless permission otherwise is given by Management. If so the private conveyance must follow that of Management's. Failure to comply to this requirement disqualifies said dog or dogs.

Rule No. 32. No person to be allowed on tracks without permission of Field Marshal, except authorized track layers.

Rule No. 33. All dogs shall be numbered on both sides, and no dog or dogs to be painted by any other than officially designated by Management.

Rule No. 34. Judges' decision will be rendered on a percentage basis, and in the event of a tie for first line or tree by two or more dogs, first and second money shall be equally divided between said dogs be it elimination, semifinal, or Final heat.

Rule No. 35. Judges' decision is final.

Rule No. 36. Upon the signature of a majority of dog handlers in any given elimination heat, a dog known to fight or interfere on trail or at tree must be muzzled or withdrawn from race. Entry fee shall be refunded if dog is withdrawn. If owner withdraws his dog or dogs entry fee shall be refunded. Protest must be made before said dog is auctioned in his heat. As the dog runs in his heat he shall run in semifinal and Finals. All dogs regularly run with muzzle on shall compete with muzzle on in all heats, semifinals and Finals.

Rule No. 37. No entry fee or nomination fee will be refunded if owner withdraws his dog or dogs. If dog is withdrawn from heat or is not present when heat is run, said dog cannot run in any other elimination or post-entry heat.

Rule No. 38. Any dog having won $40 or more in either tree or line division, regardless of whether the money is accepted or not, shall be declared a Senior dog, and cannot run as a Junior in these field trials. A combined tree and line Final when neither division totals $40 shall not graduate dog. Registered Pup Futurity winners are exempted, except when winners of a race other than a Pup Futurity Race.

Rule No. 39. Any protest on a Senior dog being run as a Junior shall be made to the Field Marshal before said dog is auctioned in his elimination heat.

Rule No. 40. When two or more dogs are voted a tie decision in a heat, they automatically contest in the same semifinal.

Rule No. 41. Tree dog is the first dog treeing to the satisfaction of the tree Judges and within an imaginary circle within the radius of the Judges' posts.

Rule No. 42. In case of a dead heat or no qualifications for tree, line, or second line in a Junior heat, that portion of auction money not qualified for shall be carried over to the next Junior heat producing a winner of that division or divisions. Senior and Green heats to be handled in same manner.

Rule No. 43. All entries will close promptly at 11:01 A.M. local time.

Rule No. 44. Management reserves the right to refuse to run post entries in any class if less than six dogs are entered in that class Post entry fee will be refunded if dogs are not run. Management reserves the right to open and close post entries as they see fit.

There are, however, times when these rules need to be varied to suit individual occasions. Therefore, it has been thought advisable to set the rules in a new order, to change them slightly, and to have these rules adopted by the coon hunters associations everywhere after they have been changed to suit the great majority of hunters who participate in field trials. The following are therefore only suggestions, for the separate clubs to pass upon.

General

1. The Coonhound Field Trials under the auspices of the ...... will be held rain or shine on .... The meet will open at ......, the first heat being run at ...... or at the option of the Management.

2. The Management reserves the right to declare these trials off in the event of insufficient entries or of weather which makes it impossible to conduct the trials, in which event nomination fees will be returned.

3. The Management is not responsible for damage suffered by any person or dog, or the property of any person attending these field trials.

4. Adequate stakes will be provided to which all dogs must be tied excepting at such times as their attendants are exercising them.

5. Dogs which are not chain broken must be constantly attended.

Prizes

1. A blue ribbon and a cash prize of $.... for each winning tree dog, and a blue ribbon and $.... for each winning line dog in each heat, will be paid. Dogs coming 2d and 3d will receive a red ribbon and a yellow ribbon respectively.

2. A blue ribbon and a cash prize of an amount equaling ⅜ of all monies collected by the nominations and entry fees shall be presented to the person entering the dog which wins the Grand Final in the tree Finals; a blue ribbon and a cash prize of one quarter of all monies collected shall be paid the winner of the line Finals. Dogs coming 2d and 3d will receive a red ribbon and a yellow ribbon respectively.

3. A silver loving cup or blue ribbon shall be given the winner of the free-for-all, and a red ribbon and a yellow ribbon will be given the winner of 2d and 3d respectively. No prizes shall be given in the semifinals.

4. In the event that two or more dogs shall be tied at either line or tree, the respective purses shall be divided between them equally and said dogs shall be eligible to enter the semifinal (or Final if no semifinal is held).

Entries

1. Nominations for the ...... Coonhound Field Trials must be in the mail before midnight ...... (The Management may decide whether or not to accept post entries. If they are to be accepted it should be

stated in advance. In that event all the nominations do is to give the club some indication of the number of entries there will be. Allowing no post entries generally greatly limits the number of dogs entered.)

2. A nomination fee of $. . . . for each dog entered shall accompany each entry. Upon the day of the trial an additional amount of $. . . . shall be paid for each entry. Payment must be in cash, no checks accepted.

3. The name, age, color, and sex of each entry must accompany the nomination and entry together with the name and address of the person entering the dog.

4. A person entering a dog need not be the owner, but in this event the name of the real owner must be stated.

5. Substitute nominations may be made up to the time of entering the dogs with the secretary prior to the running of the meet, and before the numbers have been designated to the dogs by the management.

6. All dogs admitted to the grounds are subject to an examination by a competent veterinarian. In cases of dogs exhibiting any form of infectious disease, which in the opinion of the veterinarian might endanger the health of any other entrant, such sick dogs must be immediately removed from the grounds. In such cases, the nomination fee shall be refunded. Examination shall be made before entries are accepted.

7. All dogs shall be marked by a water-soluble or easily removable nonpoisonous paint, clearly applied to both sides.

8. The person entering a dog shall be considered by

the club to be to all intents the real owner, and no discrimination shall be shown to prevent such a dog being chosen in a heat with a dog belonging to the real owner.

9. No dog may be entered more than once; no dog may compete in more than one elimination heat.

Judges

1. The Judges shall consist of three tree Judges and two line Judges.

2. The tree Judges shall stand back at a sufficient distance from the tree so that they shall not indicate to the dogs by their attitude in what tree the coon is tied. The line Judges shall stand, one at each line flag.

3. After each heat and final, the five Judges shall assemble and the two line Judges will report on which dogs ran between the flags. On the basis of this information, the tree Judges shall render a decision as to the winning dog.

4. The decision of the Judges shall be final.

5. The Judges are not to be disturbed, and all others shall stay away from them. The Judges shall not allow disputes of their decisions and may, at their discretion, debar any person from further competition, and have any person ordered from the grounds.

6. In determining the line final all five Judges shall stand at the finish line, two on one side, at a flag, and three at the other.

7. The first dog arriving at the Judge tree, which rears on or muzzles the tree, and barks up and shows to

the Judges that he knows the coon is there, will be declared the winner in each of the elimination, semifinal, or Grand Final heats.

Disqualifications

1. Any dog shall be disqualified whose owner or attendant shall have changed the marking on the dog which shall have been placed there by the secretary.

2. Any dog shall be disqualified who shall have been substituted by an owner or attendant for one that has been registered with the secretary, unless permission is given by the secretary before the substitution is made.

3. Any dog which by any manner or cause shall have been liberated at the source of the trail before the starter has given the signal to the entire field, shall be automatically disqualified and shall not be entitled to any consideration on the part of the judges.

4. The running of a heat, semifinal, or Finals in which such an event shall have occurred shall be delayed until the dog has been caught and removed from the field. All nomination and starting fees are forfeited by the person entering the dog.

5. Any dog shall be disqualified whose owner or attendant shall leash him, shall call encouragement to him or call him or in any way endeavor to indicate the location of the tree to the dog, before the judges shall have blown the whistle. Such a dog shall receive no consideration from the judges.

6. Any dog that has been withdrawn from or dis-

qualified in any elimination heat shall not be allowed to enter in another.

Heats and Semifinals

1. Numbers shall be drawn for the heats, to eliminate any favoritism, and no heat shall consist of more than eight entries. The number of heats shall be determined by the secretary in collaboration with the judges.

2. No person entering a number of dogs shall be required to have more than one dog in each heat unless the number he enters is so large that there are more dogs than the total number of heats decided upon. In that event, no more than two of his dogs shall be placed in one heat, and they shall be chosen by lot.

3. The management assumes no responsibility with relation to conditions which may arise due to the negligence or tardiness of any owner or attendant in bringing his dog to the starting post, after his name and number has been called repeatedly and posted.

4. All dogs and attendants, after having assembled at the starting post, shall become in charge of the Starter, under whose jurisdiction they shall remain until the signal has been given to start.

5. Any dog may win both tree and line finals but only tree winner will compete in the semifinals. All heats will be limited to ten minutes, starting from the moment the starter has given the signal to go! Any dog not over the line within that period of time shall not be considered in choosing the winner. In semifinal and

Final heats the time limit shall be set by the judges, who shall take into consideration the length of the course.

6. No elimination heat will be contested more than twice in order for some dog to qualify.

7. In the Grand Finals, the dogs shall be ranked in the order of First, Second, and Third Tree dogs; and one, two, three line dogs.

8. If a sufficient number of dogs are entered to make it necessary, semifinal heats shall be run. In that event, the best two dogs from each heat shall be chosen by the Judges to compete in the semifinals. In the event that the entry is small, no semifinals shall be run.

9. From the semifinals the Judges shall choose the best two tree dogs and the best two line dogs to compete in the line finals and tree finals.

10. In no event will any heat be started after darkness.

11. Females will not run against males in the elimination heats, but will contest against them in the semifinals and the GRAND FINAL with the exception that any female who becomes eligible to the semifinal will not be drawn, but will run in the last heat of the semifinals.

Courses and Trails

1. The courses shall be laid out by the committee in charge, to be called the Course Committee. It shall be the duty of said committee to decide upon the courses and to see that the trails are properly laid.

2. The length of the trail may be any distance decided upon provided that it exceeds a half mile in

length. A new trail may be laid at each heat over new ground or the same ground may be used repeatedly, with the exception of the finals, which shall be run over new ground.

3. A drag may be used or a live coon led to establish the trail or the two alternated, at the option of the Course Committee.

4. In the event that a drag is used, a live coon must be tied in the tree just as in the case where a live coon is used on a lead to lay the trail. The same coon need not be used in the tree and to lay the trail, but one coon may be tied in the tree and another used each time to lay the trail.

5. Two flags shall be placed by the Course Committee, approximately one hundred and fifty feet from the tree, and ninety feet apart, each flag being approximately equidistant from the line on which the coon was led.

6. There shall be no turns in the trail laid at any point within 300 feet of the tree.

7. A dog to qualify at the tree must have run between the flags in each elimination, semifinal, and Final heat.

8. The line dogs shall be judged at an imaginary line extending from one flag to the other. The first dog to cross this imaginary line shall be declared the winning line dog.

9. The spectators shall stand back of a point designated by the Course Committee which shall be at least fifty yards from the tree and the line.

10. The line shall be laid so that no part of it shall be closer than a quarter of a mile from the point at which the dogs not competing are tied.

11. No dogs shall be permitted to be away from the dog yard at any time while the trials are in progress. No owner or attendant will be permitted to train or exercise his dog over the course as has been adopted by the management for the elimination heats. Failure to recognize this rule automatically disqualifies said dogs.

12. No owner, spectator, or attendant shall be permitted during the progress of any heat, semifinal, or Final to approach within the limit set by the committee until the Judges have signified by the blowing of a whistle that they may do so. The whistle blown by the Head Judge shall signify that the owners or attendants may take up their dogs so that the Judges may retire to consult before rendering a decision. In the event that dogs engage in a fight, the Judges may call upon the owners or any others to come and assist in separating them.

Line Finals

1. The line Finals shall be held before the tree Finals.

2. The coon which is led, if a drag is not used, need not be placed in a tree but may be taken away immediately.

3. At a point 150 feet from the flags, which shall be 75 feet apart, the owners shall wait and catch their dogs as they come to that point and shall be caught by their owners or handlers and leashed.

4. The Judges shall declare the first, second, and third line dogs. One dog can win both tree and line money in the grand final.

Tree Finals

1. In the case of the final trial, inasmuch as measures will be taken to make it more complex than the preliminary trails, and inasmuch as a winner must be chosen, the event shall be contested over as many times as is necessary for some dog to qualify to the satisfaction of the judges.

2. The judges shall select the first, second, and third tree dogs in the finals.

3. In the event that it is possible to do so, as soon as the first dog has barked tree and established in the minds of the judges that he has won, if another dog has not yet appeared, the first shall be taken away from the tree, so as not to indicate to the next dog or dogs to arrive, the location of the coon.

Free-for-All

The grand climax to the meet shall be a free-for-all, which shall be over a trail at least a mile long. The Judges shall declare the winner. There may be a line winner at the option of the club if adequate prizes are offered.

Index

Adaptability to change, 8
Albino, 39
Appearances, daylight, 9 f.
Arakum, 3
Artificial light, indifference to, 10

Bad mating fallacy, 38
Barking, differences in, 107
Birth-marking fallacy, 38
Black-and-tan:
  breeders of, 50
  description of, 45 f.
  judging points, 52
  official A.K.C., 53 f.
  official U.K.C., 51 f.
  picture, 50
  variations of, 49
  vs. Bloodhound, 46
Bloodlines, 38
Bluetick coonhound:
  credits for preparation of standard, 60
  judging points, 65
  official U.K.C., 61 f.
  picture, 61
  purpose of standard, 61
Breeds, establishment of, 42

Cazort family, bluetick and English tricolor, 44
Characteristics, acquired, 38
Connecticut championship, 167 f.
Coon dog:
  daytime walks, 110
  differences in night and day dogs, 169
  differences in trail and sight dogs, 172
  firmness in training, 98
  general appearances, 26
  head, 27
  height, 26
  hunting by automobile, 110 f.
  keeping dog at tree, 112 f.
  legs and feet, 27
  necessity of active training, 103
  possums and porcupines, 102
  preparing coon trail, 100
  profile, 25
  rivalry in hounds, 101
  squirrel as quarry, 103, 110

Coon dog—cont'd:
  stimulating hunting desire, 100
  tail, 27
  teaching "don't touch," 99
  teaching "take it," 99
  teaching to range, 102
  training, appreciation of its importance, 98
  uses of live raccoons, 101
Coonhound, origin of, 44 f.
Coonhound, subbreeds of:
  Black-and-tan, 45
  English Bloodhound, 44
  Plott hound, 67
  Redbone, 55
  Ticked breeds, 59
  Treeing Walker, 71

Deer, break from running, 104 f.
Disease, 8
Dog, purchase of:
  buying a hound at a distance, 93
  buying with locale in mind, 93 f.
  fraud, 95
  trial period, 94
  what to avoid, 92

Electric collar, 109
English Fox and Coonhound Standard:
  judging points, 67
  official U.K.C., 65 f.
  picture, 66

Fangs, removal of, 134 f.
Field trials:
  course and trails, 201 f.
  disqualifications, 199 f.
  entries, 196 f.
  free-for-all, 204
  general rules, 195
  growing uniformity of rules and dogs, 165
  heats and semifinals, 200 f.
  judges, 198 f.
  line finals, 203 f.
  methods of, 161 f.
  necessity of clarifying competitions, 170 f.
  value of field trials, 164
  variety of entries, 163 f.
Field trial, ground arrangement:
  admission gate, 179
  flagpoles, 180
  lavatories, 180
  posting winners, 180 f.
  refuse containers, 180
  shelter and concessions, 179
  signs, 180
Field trial, manner of conducting:
  advertising suggestions, 176 f.

Field trial—cont'd:
ballyhoo, 176
clean up, 185
location and facilities, 174 f.
programs, 178
responsibility, 174
viewing entries, 178 f.
Field trial proper:
adjusting trail layout to climate, 183
announcer, 184
crossing trail, 183
laying of trail, 182
numbering of dogs, 183 f.
"pot race," 185
prizes, 196
"scent-stick," 182
Field trial runs, Standard (1951 rules):
(1) adoption of rules, 188
(2) examination of entries, 188
(3) general conduct, 188
(4) drag prescribed, 188
(5) placement of coon, 188
(6) placement of line judges, 188
(7) line flag placement, 189
(8-13) entry rules, 189 f.
(14) management of and responsibility of, 190
(15) elimination heats, 190
(16) size of heats, 190

(17) repetition of elimination heat, 190
(18) repetition of other heats, 190
(19) time of heats, 190
(20) exercise on course, 190 f.
(21) assembly, 191
(22-23) starting a heat, 191
(24) behavior on specific trail, 191
(25) prompting dog, 191 f.
(26) eligibility for semifinals or finals, 192
(27) dogs' position awaiting decision, 192
(28) change of course with heats, 192
(29) time limits, 192
(30) management assumes trail and purse responsibility, 192
(31) dogs to starting post, 193
(32) restriction of tracks, 193
(33) number of dogs, 193
(34) percentage basis of decisions, 193
(35) finality of decision, 193
(36) muzzled dogs, 193
(37) return of fee, 193 f.
(38-39) restrictions of senior dog, 193

Field trial runs—cont'd:
  (40) tie decisions, 193
  (41) definition of tree dog, 193
  (42) disposition of money in dead heat, 193
  (43) entry closing time, 193
  (44) size of class necessary, 193 f.
Field trials, tree finals, 204
Fingers as eyes, 11 f.
Fox, breaking from, 104 f.
Fox hunting, 47
Fur, 15

Habitat, cornfields, 25
Health of dog, 32
Heredity:
  chromosomes, 34
  dominant and recessive genes, 35
  examples of genes in heredity, 35
  genes, 32
  genetic expectations, 36
  germ plasm, 23
  ova (female), 34
  "skipping" a generation, 35
  sperm cells (male), 34
Heredity in the coon dog, 37
Hibernation fallacy, 15
Hunting:
  automobile method, 124
  burlap bag for, 139
  clothing for, 136 ff.
  compass for, 141 f.
  Connecticut, 22 f.
  coons, 119 f.
  Florida, 21
  Georgia, 24
  guns for, 138 f.
  lights for, 140 f.
  Maine, 19 f.
  Michigan, 21 f.
  pliers and Nembutal for, 139 f.
  ranging method, responsibility to wide ranger, 120 f.
  Texas, 23
  Virginia, 24 f.
  walking method, responsibility of hunter, 123
Hound crosses, 73 f.
  attitudes toward, 74 f.
  unsuccessful, 76
Humor, sense of, in raccoon, 9

Indians, knowledge of raccoon, 4
Inheritance through genes, 38

Johnson County, Ark., 44

Killer qualifications in dog, 28

Magazines, general outdoor:
  Chase, The, 87
  Field & Stream, 87
  Red Ranger, 87
Magazines on coonhunting:
  American Cooner, The, 86
  Bloodlines, 87
  Full Cry, 86
  Mountain Music, 86
  Redbone Trailhound
    News, 87
Mental differences, Black-
  and-tan and Foxhound,
  48
Mobility, 14
Monogamy, 9
Mutations, 39

National animal, 3
Nembutal, anesthetic agent,
  131
Noise, adjustment to, 13

Parasites, 8
Pelts:
  blue hide, 145 f.
  delay in preserving, 143 ff.
  raw hide market, 145
Perseverance of coon dog, 30
Physical power of dog, 30
Plott hound:
  description of, 67 f.
  judging points, 70 f.
  official U.K.C., 68 f.
  picture, 69

Porcupines:
  breaking new dog from,
    114
  injection into vein or ab-
    domen, 118
  quills, 116
  tending severely quilled
    dog, 116 f.
  threat to new dogs, 113 f.
  use of Nembutal, 118
Puppy, selection and feeding
  of, 88

Rabbits, breaking from, 104,
  107 f.
Raccoon:
  actions, 4
  adaptability of, 4, 6
  anesthetic method of
    catching, 131 ff.
  appearance, 4
  collaring, 133 f.
  dog-catching method,
    127 f.
  eating of, 154 ff.
  enemies in man, 7
  enemies of, 5
  food of, 5
  forked-stick catching
    method, 129 f.
  fraternization of, 7
  general impression of, 13
  hollow-tree catching
    method, 130 f.
  homes of, 5

Raccoon—cont'd:
  indiscriminate killing of, 125
  net catching method, 126 f.
  preservation of, 124 f.
  preservation of kittens, 125 f.
  protective coloring, 6
  public's idea of, 4
  recipes for preparation of, 156 ff.
  restocking hunting grounds, 125
  self-sufficiency of, 7
  size of, 6
  value of breeding rare types, 126
Ranger qualifications, 28
Rationalization, hindrance in breeding, 40
Redbone coonhound:
  general appearance, 55
  industry at hunting, 56
  official U.K.C., 57 f.
  picture, 57

Salt, use of, in stretching, 153
Scents, training and breaking agents, 108 f.
Shepherd dogs, 41

Singularity of hunting desire of dog, 30
Skinning, first method, 147 ff.; second method, 149
Socialization, 8 f.
Stretching the hide, first method, 150 f.; second method, 151 f.
Still trailer:
  advantages of, 78 f.
  cross breeding, 84
  disadvantages of, 79, 83
Swimming ability of dog, 30

Technique, fishing, 12
Ticked breeds, variations in dog, 59
Touch, sense of, 11
Training, coonhunting, 48 f.
Tree dog qualifications, 27 f.
Treeing Walker:
  description of, 71
  official U.K.C., 72 ff.
  picture, 72

Vermont Coonhunters' Association, 1943 Field Trial of, 166 f.
Vibrations, sensitivity to, 12

Washing fallacy, 11